LOVE DEEPER THAN A RIVER

Love Deeper Than a River

My Life in San Antonio

LILA BANKS COCKRELL

with Catherine Nixon Cooke

Foreword by Henry Cisneros

MAVERICK BOOKS
TRINITY UNIVERSITY PRESS
San Antonio

Published by Maverick Books,
an imprint of Trinity University Press
San Antonio, Texas 78212

Copyright © 2019 by Lila Banks Cockrell

Book design by BookMatters, Berkeley
All images appear courtesy of the author

Back cover: Photograph L-7325-047-02, San
Antonio Light Photograph Collection, UTSA Special
Collections, Institute of Texan Cultures

ISBN 978-1-59534-887-6 hardcover
ISBN 978-1-59534-888-3 ebook

Trinity University Press strives to produce its books
using methods and materials in an environmentally
sensitive manner. We favor working with manufac-
turers that practice sustainable management of all
natural resources, produce paper using recycled stock,
and manage forests with the best possible practices
for people, biodiversity, and sustainability. The press
is a member of the Green Press Initiative, a nonprofit
program dedicated to supporting publishers in their
efforts to reduce their impacts on endangered forests,
climate change, and forest-dependent communities.

The paper used in this publication meets the
minimum requirements of the American National
Standard for Information Sciences—Permanence of
Paper for Printed Library Materials, ANSI 39.48–1992.

Printed in Canada

CIP data on file at the Library of Congress

23 22 21 20 19 | 5 4 3 2 1

In memory of my beloved husband,
Sidney Earl Cockrell Jr.,
and in honor of our children

CONTENTS

FOREWORD

Henry Cisneros

In his 1998 book, Tom Brokaw bestowed the sobri-quet the "Greatest Generation" on the cohort of Americans who came of age in the years of the Great Depression and World War II. These Americans lived through the crushing economic downturn whose arrival was marked by the frightening stock market crash of 1929, and they demonstrated the grit to fight through the tumult, contraction, uncer-tainty, and personal sacrifices that characterized the 1930s. The world economy was battered, and the instability it caused soon degenerated into global political and security chaos. When the United States was pulled into the global conflagration by Japan's attack on Pearl Harbor and Germany's blitzkrieg across Europe and Africa, that same generation of Americans put on military uniforms, mastered the requirements of warfare, and fought the Axis powers to the death.

The early 1940s were years of severe hardship at

home and painful sacrifices on battlefields abroad. They were years that required courage and commitment to patriotic action. And they evoked in the Greatest Generation not only attributes of character and selflessness, but also, in the aftermath of the war, the confidence and optimism to will the United States into its essential role as the leader of the community of nations in the quest for world peace, economic prosperity, scientific advances, medical breakthroughs, and social progress. Their legacy of postwar engagement includes the United Nations, the Marshall Plan, the security umbrella of the Pax Americana, modern consumer products and services, the interstate highway system, the effective eradication of diseases such as polio and tuberculosis, the space program, and the civil rights laws. These advances and many others are the results of a collective generational effort, but they are also the products of individual commitments and beliefs.

As long as I have known Lila Cockrell, I have thought of her as a quintessential member of the Greatest Generation. Everything about her affirms her love of country and of America's core values, a sense of duty, and the resolute responsibility of the Greatest Generation. Lila knows America well. Her family roots, her experiences as a child, and her formative years in Fort Worth, New York, San Antonio, and Dallas taught her about different places, people, and public roles. Lila showed from early life the natural intelligence, lively curiosity, and well-placed confidence that would serve her in good stead throughout her life. Family life for Lila in the 1920s and 1930s was a Norman Rockwell tableau of earnestness, manners, studiousness, and growing awareness. She saw in her uncles and stepfather respect for the principles of the law and for the efficacy of public service. She excelled at Southern Methodist University and was prepared to follow in her family's footsteps of meaningful societal contributions. She realized her own substantial capabilities and began the lifelong process of diplomatically but firmly applying her prodigious capacities in an America where leadership posts were still largely reserved for men.

Lila tells the story of how she met the love of her life, Sid Cockrell, at a YWCA conference in Colorado. She recounts that after seeing him in the post office at Estes Park, she told her roommate that she had just met the man she was going to marry. It was a natural connection of two smart, service-oriented, and attractive young people. Sid had an amiable, easygoing, wholesome, all-American persona. I thought years later when I met him that he would have made a perfectly good stand-in for Jimmy Stewart in a movie role. He was definitely a major reason why Lila would be Lila in the years to come. They had an old-fashioned romance that never ended and was obvious in the mutual admiration and support they gave each other, not to mention the appreciative smiles and sweet nothings they exchanged into their seventies. After that initial meeting they courted from a distance and married in 1942, with the war in Europe and the Pacific well under way. Since Sid was already on active duty, they started married life on the post of Fort Sill, in Oklahoma.

As with many Greatest Generation couples, history intervened and personal plans were interrupted. Each of the newlyweds had officer commissions in the U.S. military, Sid as an army officer and Lila as a navy WAVES officer. Sid served as a member of a general's staff, including a tour of duty in Iceland, and Lila served in administrative positions in Washington. Both of their lives thereafter were influenced by their leadership responsibilities and by their service to the nation in that time of war.

Like other members of the Greatest Generation, Sid and Lila committed enthusiastically to peacetime pursuits as the war ended. It was a full life: Sid's career in organizational management in Dallas and

San Antonio; the birth of two daughters, Carol and Cathy; household duties, volunteer work, and civic leadership for Lila. In 1963 Lila became the first woman to serve on the San Antonio city council in a city government headed by a strong leader, Mayor Walter McAllister. It was an important time for the city, dominated by the planning and execution of HemisFair 1968. Lila observed and learned the requirements of leadership in a growing city and came to understand the rhythms and complexities of a diverse, multicultured, and historic community.

When she was urged to stand for election as mayor in 1975 and decided to enter the race, it was as if Lila had been preparing her entire life to lead a city that needed her steady and calming leadership. Every strand of confidence, knowledge, experience, and instinct from a lifetime of learning and service, of love and faith, was applied to the task at hand. She was the first woman to be elected mayor of San Antonio and the first woman mayor of a major American city. She was the first mayor directly chosen by the San Antonio electorate—as opposed to being voted in by city council members. And she was exactly what the city needed to bring civility and decorum to an era of implacable divisions, bare-knuckled politics, and swirling resentments.

Lila's tenure as mayor was a decisive time for San Antonio:

- She guided the city toward unprecedented protection of its water supply.

- She committed the city to diversified reserves of energy supplies for power generation.

- She presided over the transformation of the city's governance, introducing a new era of single-member districts that established representation for San Antonio's minority populations and disenfranchised neighborhoods.

- She advocated for diverse appointments on the city staff and on its key boards and commissions, including mentoring for women as never before.

- She supervised an unprecedented commitment to economic development and industrial attraction, in order to create jobs and fair wages and expand the city's middle class.

- She strengthened the role of the mayor's office in international relationships, particularly with Mexico, and in domestic policy discussions in Washington.

* She set an admired example of multifaceted leadership: a tenacious negotiator when necessary, a nuanced peacemaker when appropriate, a formidable political foe when called for, and the city's articulate and gracious representative always.

I had the privilege of working closely with Lila for the six years that she was mayor. In a literal sense, as the representative of District 1 on the city council, I sat next to Lila on the city council dais. As a person elected on her electoral slate in 1975, I often helped assemble the votes for her initiatives. And in the truly contentious citywide struggles of the era—such as aquifer protection, utility rate battles, and single-member districting—we coordinated continuously. It was from these experiences and recollections that I formed my convictions about her core values and her character as those of the Greatest Generation. Those character traits were visible in the daily actions and well-considered decisions of an admirable leader.

In those tumultuous years, our Thursday city council meetings would often be intense, exhausting, and frustrating political marathons lasting almost until midnight. On Friday morning I expected to see Lila exhibiting physical tiredness and emotional soreness from the previous night's political combat. Instead she was refreshed and unburdened, excited and determined to get the ship back on track. She seemed to have endless reserves of goodwill and determination. Lila Cockrell is the most irrepressibly optimistic, temperamentally steady, and inspirational can-do leader I have ever known, and that includes another world-class optimist with whom I worked, President Bill Clinton.

Frequently public issues present themselves as a solid wall of obstruction: no-win, lose-lose propositions. But Lila would keep searching, probing, listening, and trying. She is perfectly suited by personality to explore as long as it takes to find a sliver of daylight in that wall of darkness. And when she found it, she knew how to expand that sliver into a workable passageway for all of us. As mayor, Lila fought hard for San Antonio; she pushed herself hard for San Antonio. And through it all, she was scrupulously honest and unfailingly fair.

A few years ago, long after her tenure as mayor, and as her prodigious work for the Parks Foundation and her boundless civic contributions could be seen and appreciated, Lila was chosen to receive an award from a civic group for her contributions to the progress of downtown. I was honored to be asked to introduce her and present the award at the Tobin Center. After I finished my remarks from the stage, describing her many accomplishments for downtown, Lila stood up at her table to acknowledge the award. As she did, she lost her footing and fell to the floor. It was clear that she was hurt, so we paused the program and called the city's emergency medical service. An EMS team arrived quickly and within minutes diagnosed Lila's injury as a broken bone. They secured her on a gurney for the drive to the hospital. As they prepared to wheel Lila out of the hall, she asked the EMS technicians to stop. She asked for the portable microphone, propped herself up on the gurney with pillows, and proceeded to deliver a gracious, appreciative, and comprehensive speech on the importance of our downtown.

A broken femur could wait; the painkillers could wait. The emergency stabilization of her leg would have to wait. Lila wanted to thank the organizers of the event and to thank her collaborators in creating downtown progress. The audience was witness to a courageous performance by a determined leader with the physical stamina and the iron will to finish what she started. They clapped, whooped, cheered, and whistled as Lila waved goodnight en route to a waiting ambulance. It was a Greatest Generation performance worthy of MacArthur, Patton, or even Churchill.

San Antonio has been fortunate that Lila Cockrell has been our mayor—but more than that, our example, our inspiration, our North Star. Like many other people whose lives Lila has touched, I am grateful. She gave me encouragement and the latitude to pursue initiatives I felt were important to San Antonio. In the years since, I have at times reflected on where a particular approach to a problem came from or why I feel confident in the course of a negotiation, and it usually harkens back to something I learned from Lila Cockrell. Simply stated, she has been one of the most important people in my life. This is certainly true for many others—people she has mentored, women she has inspired, men who have broadened their thinking, young people who have greater opportunities, and hundreds of thousands of residents who live in a better city.

I have had the privilege of working with Lila. For readers who have not had that privilege, this book—the product of Lila's prodigious memory, of her diligent work with Catherine Nixon Cooke to share her experiences, and most importantly, of her public life of accomplishments—will uplift you with inspiration and provide you a healthy dose of Lila's trademark optimistic approach to life.

ONE

The Lure of Texas

1882–1922

When my grandmother was three years old, her parents brought her from Kentucky to Texas in a covered wagon, bumping along more than 1,000 miles of rough paths and open country on a journey that must have taken three months, perhaps longer if rains were heavy that year. Promises of great opportunities in what was then the largest state in the union had lured William and Maude Hamilton to pack up everything they owned in Foster, in Bracken County—including little Julia and her older brother, and a huge supply of courage—and to endure the journey in 1882 to the small town of Hockley, not far from what is now the booming city of Houston, Texas. Eventually this toddler would become my grandmother and my heroine, my role model of a strong, independent woman who could achieve anything she set out to do. Family stories confirm that she "took charge" of my birth in 1922, and I know firsthand that she continued to shape my growth and development for the rest of her life.

I am certain that her early days on the trail to Texas led to her can-do spirit, and although formal education in her new hometown only went to the fourth grade in the 1880s, her active, inquisitive mind prepared her for the important role she would play in our family and beyond. While Hockley did not live up to the glowing descriptions that had convinced William Hamilton to buy farmland there sight unseen, the family made the best of their new life in Texas, and by the time Julia was in her teens, electricity and running water brought a bit of modernity to their small town.

In 1899, when she was twenty years old, my grandmother married Elliott Tompkins, who came from a distinguished family that moved from Alabama to Hempstead, Texas, in 1874. The groom's grandfather, Henry Clay Clark Tompkins, was born in 1827 in Franklin County, Alabama, the eldest of ten children. He married Martha Jones Gladish and moved with his family in 1874 to Gladish, Texas, which was founded by his wife's family. They had ten children, including Arthur Clark Tompkins, who married Westchina Norwood in 1876 and moved in 1881 to

My grandmother, Julia Hamilton, came to Texas in a covered wagon. Her strong character was a major influence in my life.

Hempstead, where he practiced law. He served as a member of the Texas 17th Legislature in 1881–82 and the 24th Legislature in 1894–96 and held other various elected offices. Perhaps my great-grandfather's genes influenced my love of government. Arthur and Westchina Tompkins had six children; Elliott was the eldest.

After Elliott and Julia married, they settled in Hempstead. My mother, Velma Tompkins, was born on December 8, 1900. Her little brother, Arthur, followed in 1904; sadly, he passed away not long before his fifth birthday. My grandmother did not share much about her early married life with Elliott, but she never forgot the sadness she felt when her young son died from illness, all too common in those days before antibiotics. Her marriage must not have been very happy, because she divorced her husband—an unusual action for a woman living in those times—for what she later described to us as "biblical reasons."

As a single, divorced woman in the early 1900s, my grandmother supported herself by turning her home into a small hotel. It was located close to the railroad station, and in order to attract paying guests, she hired a porter, who met arriving trains at the station. The porter would approach a passenger who was disembarking, frequently a traveling salesman, and say, "May I carry your bags to the hotel, sir?" The arriving traveler would then be taken to my grandmother's hotel.

Andrew McCampbell was one of those travelers. He was attracted to the beautiful hotel owner, and after a formal courtship they married in Hempstead on December 12, 1912. He had held several government positions, including serving as a federal marshal. Fort Worth must have been his home, because that is where the newlyweds and my twelve-year-old mother moved. Andrew McCampbell proved to be a fine gentleman and husband, a devoted stepfather to my mother and, in future years, a wonderful grandfather to me.

My mother graduated from high school in Fort Worth and enrolled at the College of Industrial Arts, which later became Texas Woman's University, in nearby Denton. She was a popular student, enjoying college life, although the war being fought in Europe had begun to inflame the passion and compassion of American citizens. As early as 1915, after the Germans sank the *Lusitania,* our country had begun building up its military forces for defensive purposes. In April 1917 the United States joined World War I.

My mother and some of her college friends attended dances with the young soldiers stationed at

Julia Velma

My grandmother Julia remarried in 1912, and my mother, twelve-year-old Velma Tompkins, got a wonderful new stepfather.

Camp Bowie in Fort Worth; she met my father at one of those parties. Robert Bruce Banks was a young attorney from San Antonio, commissioned as a first lieutenant after graduation from officer's training school at Leon Springs. Soon after my parents met and fell in love, my father was shipped overseas as part of the 35th Division, 143rd Infantry Regiment. He was quickly promoted to captain and served in France as the regimental adjutant.

My father wrote detailed letters to his mother and to his sweetheart. They reveal a thoughtful, well-educated man, and they give us such a clear picture of what war was like in the early 1900s.

Hq. 143rd Inf.
American Ex. Forces, APO 796
FRANCE, 17 Oct., 1918

Dear Mamma:

I have a little more time today as things are somewhat quieter on the front—so I am writing you another letter which I hope will reach you in due course. I am going to tell you a few things which I think will not violate any of the censorship rules. As we were advancing, some of the boys looked into a German dugout and found written in English, "We are on the way to the Fatherland—follow us if you can." We found the Germans had gone back very rapidly. The roads were in good condition, very few trees were cut down, and only [one] or two of the towns had been fired. There were all kinds of material on the ground—rifles, ammunition, helmets, clothing, mess kits, everything imaginable. I am going to try to get a few souvenirs to send home. How would you like to have a German helmet?...Before we got quite to the line, I spent a night some six or seven miles behind. I made up my bed in a shell hole, and was just getting to sleep when Fritz began to throw high explosive shells in our direction. We could hear them whistle over our heads, and on either side of us. Nearly everyone made for a dugout, but I was too sleepy and just staid [*sic*] in my shell hole. Luckily none of the shells hit close in there. But all along the territory over which we advanced there were many dead bodies—Germans, French, and Americans. You soon get accustomed to such sights, for such is war...and airplane fights are as numerous as cat fights in the alley on a dark night.

When the war ended, my father returned and proposed to my mother. They were married at the Prospect Hill Methodist Church in San Antonio in 1919, with members of both families and close friends in attendance. As my mother became acquainted

My uncle, Stanley Banks (*left*), and father, Robert Bruce Banks (*right*), were both attorneys who served in World War I.

with her husband's family, she discovered its long and interesting history.

My paternal grandfather, Edwin Gray Banks, was born in 1842 in Clinton, Mississippi, the oldest of eight children. He was educated at Mississippi College and later taught there as a professor of Latin and Greek. He enlisted in the Confederate army in 1861 and was wounded in the Battle of Fredericksburg, in Virginia. When the war ended, he moved to Seguin, Texas, where he taught school and studied law. In 1871 he married Mollie Granbery, and they had one son, Edwin Gray Banks Jr., in 1878. In those days before modern medicine, illnesses like diphtheria and influenza were not curable, and both Mollie and her baby son died not long after the birth. My grandfather moved to neighboring Caldwell County, where he served as county judge for many years, and in 1881 he married his second wife, Lila Caroline Edwards. They had eight children together, including my father in 1895. The family moved to Lufkin around the turn of the century, and my father graduated from high school there before attending the University of Texas at Austin.

In 1911 the Banks family moved to San Antonio because its youngest member, Anna, had contracted tuberculosis, which was rampant and deadly in those days. San Antonio had a treatment center—the Santa Rosa Infirmary. One of only nineteen hospitals in Texas, it was established in 1869 by the Sisters of Charity of the Incarnate Word; its pediatric unit opened in the late 1800s, and it employed some of the best-trained doctors and nurses in the state.

The family's first home was in the growing Prospect Hill area of San Antonio. Just west of downtown, it was an ethnically diverse community of working families and local businesses, one square mile in size. Many of the early families living there were associated with the railroad, which had added San Antonio to its route in 1878. Prospect Hill was also on one of the early streetcar lines, and by the time the Banks family moved there, it was known for its modern ambience.

Over the years many well-known characters grew up in Prospect Hill, including Lionel Sosa, founder of the largest Hispanic advertising agency in the United States; Dr. Fernando Guerra, who directed the San Antonio Metropolitan Health District for twenty-three years; Hope Andrade, former Texas secretary of state; Henry Cisneros, former mayor of San Antonio and HUD secretary; actress Carol Burnett; the Cortez family, owners of Mi Tierra, Pico de Gallo, and La Margarita; Tessa Martinez Pollack,

The Banks family lived in a large house in Lufkin, Texas, before moving to San Antonio in 1911. My father, Bruce, is pictured on the far left.

who was president of Our Lady of the Lake University; and nationally acclaimed artist Jesse Treviño.

The Banks children were well educated and pursued successful careers. Both my father and his brother Stanley became attorneys; Lucy earned a master's degree from Columbia University and became an education supervisor in San Antonio's largest school district; and Frances became a teacher at Crockett Elementary School.

After my parents were married in 1919, they lived downtown in the Morning Glory Apartments. A few years later they bought a home in the more elegant Laurel Heights neighborhood, which had a new electric streetcar route that connected to a growing downtown. My father rode the streetcar to his office in the Crockett Building, at the corner of Losoya and Crockett Streets, where he worked as an attorney in the office of Chandler and Company, a land title and abstract firm. His brother, C. Stanley Banks, joined the company as well, and for many years he served as a trustee for the Chandler estate, which included the beautiful family home on West French Place designated by the Chandler family to become a residence for "impoverished gentlewomen."

The Chandlers, of course, were far from impoverished, and my mother used to tell me about wonderful tea parties she attended, hosted by Mrs. Chandler, who always wore elegant hats and white gloves. The Chandlers gave my parents an exquisite silver tea service as a wedding gift, and the tea party tradition continued into the next generations.

In spring 1921 Mother realized that she was expecting a child. Although my parents lived in

My parents, Bruce and Velma Banks, married after
World War I, in 1919.

San Antonio, my maternal grandmother, Julia May McCampbell, insisted that my mother come stay with her in Fort Worth a few weeks before my birth so that she could be "in charge" of all the arrangements. Dr. T. G. Rumph, the family's doctor, lived next door and would preside over the delivery.

My mother told me that on the evening before my arrival, she attended a patriotic concert by the John Philip Sousa band that was especially rousing. I have always thought that perhaps that patriotic prelude to my birth may have been a factor in later years, when I served in the WAVES in World War II as a company commander and marched in step with the military band as we performed in Washington, DC. Even today when our Air Force Band of the West, stationed at Lackland Air Force Base in San Antonio, strikes up a Sousa march like "The Stars and Stripes Forever," my feet start tapping and I have an urge to get up and march!

I think my love of country may have started in the womb, and on January 19, 1922, the day after the concert, I was born at All Saints Hospital in Fort Worth. My mother and father brought me home to San Antonio, where we settled into our life as a family of three. I knew from my earliest days that my grandmother would always play an important role in my growth and development in the years ahead.

Parenting and homemaking skills became my mother's primary focus, but she still found time to volunteer with the Bluebirds, a service-oriented organization at the Laurel Heights Methodist Church, where I was christened Lila May Banks in honor of my two grandmothers. Over the next few years, as various members of the Banks family moved from their homes in Prospect Hill to Laurel Heights and Beacon Hill, they became very active in the church as well. Aunt Lucy Banks provided piano accompaniment, my grandmother taught Sunday school, and Uncle Stanley served as a church officer and later helped write the history of Laurel Heights Methodist Church.

These were happy days. On special occasions the entire Banks family would enjoy breakfast parties in the Japanese Tea Garden on the San Antonio River, constructed by the city after World War I. In the 1920s a local Japanese American artist, Kimi Eizo Jingu, was invited to take up residence in the garden with his family, to help design and construct its lush planting, shaded walkways, stone bridges, and ponds filled with koi fish. It was an exotic place, located on the edge of the more-than-300-acre Brackenridge

I was christened Lila May Banks.

Park, comprised of land donated by philanthropist George Brackenridge in 1899 and expanded by Emma Koehler's addition of land in 1915. My parents would have been surprised to know that more than fifty years later, this special place would become an important part of my work as president of the San Antonio Parks Foundation.

My mother experienced a wondrous surprise shortly after my birth, when my father bought one of the first automobiles in the neighborhood—a 1922 Ford Model T. Just before bedtime, if I was fretful, my parents would put me in the car and take me for a ride, soothing me to sleep as they explored the neighborhoods under construction, all with paved streets, evidence of the city's modernization. San Antonio's population had increased to more than 165,000. The city had recovered from its terrible flood of the year before and was building a modern dam to prevent future disasters. Natural gas was discovered in South Texas; the first radio station, WOAI, began broadcasting news and music; and plans were under way for the construction of the Majestic Theatre and a skyscraper that would become the state's tallest office building. I was a brand-new part of a city on the rise, never dreaming that tragedy was looming on my horizon.

TWO

Loss and New Beginnings

1923–39

Yellow jaundice, a disease that would eventually be called hepatitis, took the life of my father when I was just eighteen months old. My mother was devastated, of course, and she saved the beautiful eulogy from his funeral, handwritten and signed by the minister, Caspar S. Wright. It talks about a young man of great character and promise, and every time I read it, I regret not having had the privilege of truly knowing my father.

As a friend, neighbor, brother, and as an official in the Methodist Church, it was, that I knew Bruce. In many conversations with him on almost every subject of interest to the thoughtful, I had come to estimate him highly as a man of strong and original thought, not simply in his chosen profession, but with regard to fundamental truth relating to the great future. He was candid, patient, and thorough in all his investigation. Questions which duty required him to consider and settle with regard to his Christian experience were met with the high calm courage that moved him in all walks of life. . . . Loved ones, all, there is no doubt a positive pleasure in certain forms of grief, and I cannot refrain from giving expression to my great pleasure and joy as I note that true manhood which was so greatly illustrated and is now glorified in Bruce.

> Rev. Caspar S. Wright,
> Laurel Heights Methodist Church,
> August 1923

Now a young widow with a small child, Mother decided that we would join her parents in Omaha, Nebraska, where my grandfather was in charge of the Prohibition Service office. Today memories about Prohibition and the dramas surrounding it have faded, but in 1920, when the 18th Amendment of the U.S. Constitution established the prohibition of alcoholic beverages, it was in the spotlight. The production, transport, and sale of alcohol were illegal, and the accompanying Volstead Act set down methods for enforcing the new law. My grandfather was right in the middle of that drama, first in New York City, then in Omaha, and finally back in New

York in 1926, where he was the assistant prohibition service director.

I was four years old when we moved into our apartment on Riverside Drive, and I remember lovely walks with my mother and grandparents, Muddie and Pappy, exciting visits to the Metropolitan Museum of Art, the Museum of Natural History, and the zoos in Central Park and the Bronx. I was very fond of Riverside Park. It was a linear park, bordering the Hudson River, and during our walks I was treated to little boxes of Sun-Maid raisins sold by roving vendors. About that time Mother began to receive the attentions of a handsome gentleman named Ovid Winfield Jones, who began to accompany us on the walks. He courted us both, patronizing the raisin vendor to gain favor with the daughter of the lady he hoped to marry. As the recipient of these special favors, I naturally thought he was a very nice man!

A native of Winston-Salem, North Carolina, Ovid Jones was working in the legal section of the U.S. Treasury Department. He had received his bachelor's degree from Guilford College, his master's degree from the University of North Carolina, and his law degree from Columbia University. He and Mother were married in 1927, when I was five years old, and he became not only Mother's new husband but my new daddy.

There were some interesting similarities between the stepfather who raised me and my birth father. Both men had October birthdays, both were eleven years older than my mother, both were attorneys, and both had strong, matriarchal mothers who were born in January very close to my own birthday.

After the wedding, our little family lived in a rented apartment in Forest Hills, on Long Island, but eventually purchased a two-story brick row house there. Downstairs was an entrance hall, living room, dining room, and kitchen; there were three bedrooms and one bath on the second floor. The furnace, coal bin, and some laundry facilities and storage space were in the basement. The house was not large, especially compared to the rambling frame house with wraparound porches where the Jones family lived in North Carolina. Mother told me that when relatives visited from Winston-Salem, if she referred to our home as a house, they thought of it as small, but if she called it an apartment, they tended to be impressed.

My grandparents moved to an apartment in Kew Gardens, just a short distance from our house, and in 1930 Grandfather was named prohibition director of New York and Puerto Rico. He was frequently in

My grandfather, Andrew McCampbell, was honored in 1928 for his work as the prohibition director in New York and Puerto Rico.

the news, and not always in a favorable light, because Prohibition was becoming increasingly out of favor with the public. During the entire time he served in that capacity, Grandfather was aware of being followed everywhere, never knowing if it was the security agent assigned by the government to protect him, or someone employed by bootleggers to try to find something damaging about him that could be used to blackmail or intimidate him.

My grandmother supported her husband's work and became a leader in the Woman's Christian Temperance Union. She even recruited me into the Loyal Temperance Legion when I was about eight years old. I "signed the pledge" to abstain from any use of beverage alcohol—and I kept the pledge until college days.

My grandparents' influence also inspired me to organize a neighborhood parade in support of Herbert Hoover for president in 1928. They were devoted Republicans, and they helped me purchase small flags and create signs for my recruits to wave as we marched around the neighborhood. I had saved my allowance of twenty-five cents a week to purchase several small drums so that the parade would not go unnoticed. As I was later to learn, however, none of the parents of my parade participants supported the election of Hoover, and one by one my loyal recruits were withdrawn from the parade. Soon I was left standing all alone with my signs, flags, and drums. I learned early not to be deterred by political setbacks and felt vindicated when Hoover won the presidency that year.

I entered that arena again two years later, again displaying my loyalty to my grandparents' opinions, when I wrote an ardent poem extolling the virtues of Prohibition and lamenting the efforts under way to repeal the 18th Amendment. I mailed the poem to Franklin D. Roosevelt, the governor of New York, who was a leading advocate for repeal. He responded in a very gracious manner with a letter that is now one of my prized personal treasures.

In his diplomatic response, he complimented my poem, on which he could see I had worked hard, but pointed out that while we both supported the cause of temperance, we favored different ways to achieve it. His response did not win him any points with my grandparents, but I still have the letter, and again, it is a firsthand lesson in diplomacy.

I was delighted when two little brothers came along about this time. Ovid Winfield Jones Jr. was born in 1928, and Andrew McCampbell Jones was born two years later. Little Ovid was a beautiful child, with blond hair and big blue eyes. Eleanor Enola Rockwell, a local artist in Forest Hills, won first place in a New York art show with her portrait of my brother. Ovid was the apple of my daddy's eye, and with the six-year difference in our ages, I was a doting big sister.

Evelyn Rockwell, the sister of the artist who painted Ovid, taught drama in Forest Hills in a house on Deepdene Road that seemed magical to me as a little girl. The basement had been converted into a children's theater, with a large room filled with racks of costumes, including beautiful dresses for princesses, scary clothes for witches, and assorted outfits for other female characters. There were also suits for princes, villains, and goblins, and animal costumes with extraordinary headpieces. Another large room housed a performing stage with a big seating area for parents and other patrons. Rockwell had painted all of the walls with scenes from favorite fairy tales—"Cinderella," "Goldilocks and the Three Bears," and "Hansel and Gretel." I loved going there for drama lessons and was even chosen as an extra in the Broadway children's performance of *Tom and the Water Babies.* Yes, I was one of the water babies!

As happy as my childhood was, like all families in the early 1930s, we were affected by the Great Depression that followed the stock market crash of 1929. My stepfather did not lose his job, as so many people did, but all Treasury Department employees were put on half-pay. I realize it must have been a stressful time for everyone, but Mother seemed to keep smiling and to "carry on and cope." We ate lots of spaghetti-and-meat-sauce suppers, macaroni and cheese, fresh vegetables; for dessert we had Jell-O. Our standard Sunday night dinner was milk toast, which Mother served in a beautiful covered silver casserole dish that had been a wedding present. Because of the wonderful presentation, I always regarded milk toast as a special treat.

She used that same gift for presentation whenever guests came to our house for tea. She would bring out her Japanese tea cart and the silver service that Mrs. Chandler had given her, with the teapot filled with steaming tea, the sugar bowl filled with cubes of sugar, and the little silver pitcher filled with cream. She would also have lemon slices with cloves and a silver tray of cinnamon toast. Since I watched her making all of these preparations in the kitchen before her guests arrived, I always associated cinnamon toast with absolute elegance.

For my ninth birthday, my parents arranged some unforgettable party entertainment. Fred Knight, their friend and an amateur magician, performed some amazing tricks to the delight of us all. I was fascinated and watched closely to see if I could uncover some of his secrets. For quite a while, I thought I would grow up to be a magician. And indeed sometimes politics requires some of those special skills.

Despite the Depression, I have happy memories of my childhood. Our parents took my brothers and me on some family visits to North Carolina and

Texas. Dad's family homestead was on Cherry Street near downtown Winston-Salem, and Grandmother Jones lived there with her widowed daughter, Aunt Ida Fox, whose two sons, Haywood and Billy, were about my age. They kept chickens in the backyard and had a vegetable patch as well. During the Depression, Aunt Ida, who was a marvelous cook, baked fancy cakes for restaurants and hotels to supplement their family's income, and we always looked forward to fried chicken dinners when we went to visit.

We also made trips to Texas to visit my maternal great-grandmother, Maude Hamilton, who lived in San Antonio with her daughter and son-in-law, Aunt Annie and Uncle Bob Caudle. We also visited my Banks family relatives there—Grandmother Lila Caroline Banks, Aunt Lucy and Aunt Frances, and Uncle Stanley and Aunt Annie. It was fun to stay in touch with my cousins Stanley Jr., Eleanor, John, and Mary Jo, and visits to beautiful Brackenridge Park and the zoo, where my brothers rode donkeys, were a highlight of our trips to San Antonio in the 1930s.

In 1933 Franklin D. Roosevelt took office as president, having defeated Herbert Hoover's bid for reelection, and the 18th Amendment, which established Prohibition, was repealed. My grandfather, who had supported Prohibition both personally

Visits to Texas to see my Banks family in the 1930s were always special. My little brothers, Ovid (*left*) and Andrew (*right*), loved to ride the donkeys in Brackenridge Park and pretend they were cowboys.

and politically, resigned from government service
on July 1. He and my grandmother decided to move
back to Fort Worth to take over the management
of the Les Trois apartment complex, which they
had invested in several years before. It was a complex of three buildings, with a lovely courtyard and
sixteen apartments. My grandparents lived in a large
two-bedroom unit.

Muddie and Pappy played a very important role
in my life as a child, and I really missed them when
they moved away from Forest Hills. But some
wonderful preteen adventures in New York were
happily distracting. Invitations to the legendary
Shelter Island estate of Otto Kahn, the German-born
American banker, art collector, and philanthropist,
were arranged through Mother's friendship with the
wife of Mr. Kahn's personal secretary. I remember
collecting some beautiful shells along the shore there.
When I was about eleven or twelve, I joined other
young people at the National Lawn Tennis Association's annual championship matches at the West Side
Tennis Club. We received free admission passes on
the first couple of days of the matches, to help boost
attendance in the stands, and that lesson in crowd
building proved valuable later on. I became an expert
at recognizing all the tennis players and tracking their

matches. Later, as a teenager, my picture appeared in *Newsweek* with a caption that described me as "an obstacle" on the way to the tennis courts, stopping tennis stars to get their autographs in black ink on my ivory denim jacket.

Fourth of July was especially exciting in Forest Hills. It was celebrated all day long, with town criers dressed in colonial costumes opening the festivities at 8 a.m.; they moved through town and stopped on corners to read a proclamation for the celebration of Independence Day, starting with "Hear ye, hear ye." At 10 a.m. a Broadway actor read the Declaration of Independence in Greenway Park, and the day's events proceeded with morning relay races, burlap bag races, and other games for young children, followed by afternoon recitals featuring children from the studios of local dance teachers. An Independence Ball was held at the community house in the evening, and grownups wore their finest formal attire.

Our family participated in all of these events. I can remember bumping along in the burlap race and dancing in Olivia Park with my ballet class. As my brothers grew, they too took their turns with those burlap bags, although at first Ovid's participation was not as enjoyable as it could have been, because of health problems.

He suffered from terrible earaches as a child, and I remember many distressing nights when he woke up crying in pain, with Mother and Daddy being terribly distraught. In those days there were no antibiotics for ear infections, and the mastoid bone behind the ear often became infected too. Surgery was the only answer, and thankfully, after a double mastoid operation when he was six or seven, Ovid's pain finally went away. Today antibiotics probably would have cleared up his first infection, and he would not have had to endure those years of sleepless nights.

There were fun nights too. Forest Hills celebrated Christmas by having Santa visit each home with young children, carrying a sack of gifts from which he drew out a present for each child in the family. The Santa was always a volunteer father, and quite a few were needed to cover all the homes in the community. I still remember the time Santa called at our home, not long after I had become a skeptic. My young friends and I had been having a discussion about whether Santa was real, and after carefully scrutinizing the Santa who arrived, I said, "You're Daddy!" and pulled off his beard. That was the last time Santa called at our house, and I've always regretted ruining the fun for my brothers.

Because I had received a double promotion in

elementary school, I was eleven years old when I was ready to enter eighth grade. My grandparents invited me to start living with them in Fort Worth during the school years, with a plan to spend the summers in Forest Hills. Some of my friends were entering private school at that time, but with money still tight in our family, this was not an option for me, and my grandparents' invitation seemed like a wonderful alternative to the big Jamaica public high school in Queens. I was happy with the decision because I missed my grandparents, none of my good friends were going to the local public high school, and I had always liked Texas. In fall 1933 I enrolled at Jennings Avenue Junior High School, which had previously been the high school my mother attended. I signed up for a full schedule of academics and participated in the Interscholastic League's declamation contest, winning first place for my recitation of Lincoln's soliloquy from "John Brown's Body" by Stephen Vincent Benét. That first success inspired my continued interest in speech competitions and debate through high school and college. I believe those skills are crucial in life, especially in a life in politics.

When I traveled to Forest Hills to spend the summers with my parents and brothers, I made the trip alone by train, in a luxury Pullman car, with a change of trains in Saint Louis. At age twelve I was "put under the care of the conductor" at my grandmother's insistence. I was a bit chagrined, sure that I could have handled everything by myself!

I returned to Texas each fall for school, and in 1935 I entered the tenth grade at Central High School, just a few blocks from my grandparents' apartment. I was thirteen, making new friends, and excited to be in senior high school. We were active at the First Methodist Church, and I was happily involved in youth programs there. We always went to Simpson's Dining Room after church for Sunday dinner. I remember wonderful, bountiful dinners served family style with heaping platters of food, accompanied by yummy homemade hot rolls, and they cost only thirty-five cents a person. My grandparents were always careful to leave a ten-cent tip after dinner. It is interesting to think about how the value of money has changed over the past eighty years.

About this time my grandfather's health began to concern us all. He was still busy communicating with old friends from the Prohibition service, and he received a cordial note from former president Hoover at Christmas, but his heart was failing. He passed away in June 1936, and I felt his loss keenly. A newspaper article in the *Fort Worth Star-Telegram* called him a "friend of five presidents." Looking back, I'm certain that the intense interest my grandparents had in governmental issues and politics was a catalyst in my own development. As the years went on, I would hear many different views on issues and politics, and I would remember that my grandparents' civic passion had prepared me for becoming a caring and participating citizen.

The summer that my grandfather died, Muddie stayed in Fort Worth to manage the apartment complex, and I returned to Long Island. Our family belonged to the Atlantic Beach Club, and sometimes we went to Jones Beach—a new attraction in those days and now the most popular beach on the East Coast, with more than 6 million visitors a year.

My grandmother was a strong, forceful woman who had fought for her rights and championed causes her entire life. My mother had some of those same leadership qualities, but they were modified. Mother was active in her church, and she focused more on social graces and social life. She had a lively personality and loved to entertain friends, even during the Depression. I loved watching my mother's tea parties, when she used her beautiful silver tea service and the ladies all wore pretty, long dresses and nibbled on cinnamon toast.

When I returned to school in Fort Worth the next fall, Central High School was renamed Paschal High School in honor of Robert Lee Paschal, who was principal there in the early 1900s. I continued my studies, began participating in debate, and was one of the organizers of the Little Congress, a girls' club that served as our equivalent of the Senate, a prestigious boys' organization. I had my first dates. Boys who were special to us were called beaux in those days. Richard Flowers was one of my first beaux, followed by Howard Taylor. I remember how embarrassed I was when our senior annual was published and under my picture were the words "Oh Richard" when I was no longer dating him.

On the home front, I was recruited to pick out pecans for my grandmother, who worked for many weeks making a variety of handmade candies for Christmas presents. She also baked fresh coconut cakes, which meant I had to pick out the coconut from the shell, then grind it and place it on top of the fluffy white frosting. It was a tedious task, but the cakes were delicious!

During my senior year in high school, my grandmother, mother, and I talked about where I should go to college. Because of my double promotion in elementary school and the full load I took in high

Dating—with little brothers watching—was as difficult in the 1930s as it is today.

school, I would have enough credits to graduate from high school in 1937 when I was fifteen. I put off taking my required senior English class until the following year, to postpone graduation until I was sixteen. Because I was still younger than most in my class, a family decision was made for me to attend a junior college that accepted only women for my first year away from home. I was comfortable with the decision, and in fall 1938 I entered Ward-Belmont in Nashville, Tennessee.

Ward-Belmont was a very traditional girls' finishing school with strict rules. We were required to wear a hat and gloves on any occasion when we planned to leave the campus. As for our social life, the school arranged quarterly dances with selected men in attendance, and they were carefully chaperoned. These rather formal events ended at 10 p.m. On those rare occasions when we might be lucky enough to have a date—usually with a Vanderbilt University student we had met at an earlier school dance—we were required to double-date and travel to our destination by taxicab, accompanied by a chaperone. The curfew for these outings was also 10 p.m., and those strict rules did not enhance our dating opportunities.

Each girl received an invitation to become a member of a social club, and I got my first preference, the Twentieth Century Club. Its members were known as the TCs, and we had a small "house" where we held meetings and parties. For my seventeenth birthday on January 19, 1939, Mother came to Nashville to host a party for me at the TC clubhouse. She contacted Haywood Fox, Dad's nephew, who was then a tobacco buyer for Reynolds Tobacco Company and living in the Nashville area. Haywood rounded up five other young men to serve as dates for my TC "sisters" who were invited to the party. Mother provided snacks, birthday cake, and soft drinks, and everyone was having a great time. At about 9:45 p.m. the campus security officer stuck his head in the door to remind us of the 10 p.m. curfew. Mother was on her hands and knees sweeping cigarette butts into the fireplace, having completely forgotten that as chaperone she was not supposed to permit anyone to smoke. Of course, all the young men had done just that. The security guard looked around and asked where the chaperone was. When he learned it was my pretty, young mother, all he could say was, "Well, you don't look like a chaperone to me!"

One of the challenges of attending Ward-Belmont was the need to remember not to overindulge in the delectable southern cuisine, complete with supremely tempting desserts, served in abundance in the dining room. A number of girls took up smoking in the hope that cigarettes would curb their appetites. They were permitted to smoke only in a designated room. I bought a package of cigarettes and, after smoking one or two, decided I did not like them and threw the pack away. I never had to quit in later years when we all learned that smoking was a health hazard.

Since most homes and businesses burned soft coal in Nashville, the air quality was another problem at Ward-Belmont. The coal dust seeped into everyone's clothing as well. I remember Mother's dismay when I came home for Christmas vacation and my nice college wardrobe was dingy looking—a challenge for the cleaners.

One of my suitemates, Virginia Jones, was from Louisville, Kentucky. Her father owned Jones Apothecaries, with stores all around Louisville. He also was a top official at Churchill Downs. Mr. Jones always purchased several boxes at the Kentucky Derby, and Virginia and her suitemates were invited to attend. We were on limited allowances, so we each confined our betting to pitching in fifty cents on a $2 ticket for each race. At that time, Eddie Arcaro was a very popular and successful jockey, and our betting was frequently guided as much by the jockey as by the horse. We always bet on the favorite "to show," and we frequently came up with a winning ticket, netting each girl about five cents profit on each winning bet. Mr. Jones saw to it that we were invited to a lovely reception, and I sampled my first mint julep, accompanied by open-faced cucumber sandwiches, at that elegant party.

In spring 1939, as my year at Ward-Belmont was drawing to a close, I had made plans to return to Texas in the fall to attend Southern Methodist University. As we packed up for our return to our

A small all-girls school, Ward-Belmont Junior College was a protective introduction to college life, with a wonderful spring festival.

families, we said good-bye with lots of hugs and a few tears. I had done some much-needed growing up at Ward-Belmont, and I was now prepared to enter a university.

That summer the New York World's Fair opened in Flushing Meadows, not far from our home, with the theme Building the World of Tomorrow. It was the second-largest world's fair in history, exceeded only by the Louisiana Purchase Exposition in 1904. Thirty-three countries participated and 44 million people attended. Albert Einstein gave a scientific talk that focused on cosmic rays, and President Roosevelt's speech was broadcast on the first television sets, on display in the RCA pavilion. Images appeared almost magically before the astonished in a room filled with five-inch screens, with one screen that was a whopping twenty-four inches wide.

My brother Andrew was a precocious nine-year-old, and he wanted to go to the fair at every opportunity. He begged adults in the family and even our out-of-town visitors to take him, and he collected information from every booth to study. When the fair reopened in 1940, he could have been a tour guide except for the fact that he was only ten years old. The avant-garde Queens Museum is now located on the World's Fair site.

Andrew's intense intellectual curiosity continued as he moved into adulthood, and he graduated from Dartmouth and earned a master's degree from Wichita University and a doctorate in theoretical physics from Texas Christian University.

As a big sister, I loved my brothers most of the time. But when I was starting to have dates, they would hide in the staircase to the second floor, just out of sight of the living room where I would be entertaining a young man. Sitting there very quietly, they would eavesdrop on our conversation. Then at the earliest opportunity, those little rascals would go into great detail about what my date and I had talked about, giggling with delight. My love for them was sorely tested!

THREE

Love at First Sight

1940–42

As the new decade began, I plunged into college life at Southern Methodist University in Dallas. Sororities and fraternities played a big role at the university, but Greek life was a bit different than it is today. There were no sorority residence houses at SMU, so all female students lived in the women's dormitories, where we had a chance to make friends with a diverse group of women who were members of other sororities, as well as independents. Sororities and fraternities rented small cottages that served as their headquarters and meeting rooms. I pledged Delta Delta Delta ("Tri-Delt"), whose members seemed to excel in music and sports. The beautiful voices of my music major sisters ensured that we usually won the university's singing contests. My own prowess in archery and table tennis contributed to our success in the intramural sports contests. One year we won first-place trophies in seven

At Southern Methodist University, I joined the Tri-Delt sorority in 1940. Those sisters became lifelong friends.

out of the ten competitions! Of course, as pledges we had to maintain our academic standing, and I had some outstanding professors who were wonderful mentors. My favorite was the debate coach, Dr. A. Q. Sartain, and I have thought of him often in the last seven decades of my political career as I participated in hundreds, if not thousands, of debates. Although I had never been particularly attracted to science courses, I signed up to take geology from Dr. Claude Albritten, along with half of the coeds in school, because we all thought he was so good-looking!

SMU had an all-men's cheerleading squad that rallied crowds during the fall football season. During my sophomore year, a surprising change occurred. The head cheerleader, Lucas Gariputto, invited three women to serve as guest cheerleaders for homecoming weekend, and I was so excited to be one of them. Of course, our activities were carefully monitored by the very dignified dean of girls, Dr. Lide Spraggins, who was not thrilled with the idea of women cheerleaders. Our chosen uniforms, in the SMU colors of red and blue, could not be too short or too revealing or allow our skirts to fly up too high while we were jumping around. Dr. Spraggins also made it clear that our tenure as cheerleaders could not extend beyond homecoming weekend. It would be nearly a decade before the university had full-time women cheerleaders, but we may have set the idea in motion, and as we all know, the uniforms have changed considerably over the last seventy years.

Gatherings of good friends, bridge games, late-night discussions about school, boyfriends, food in the dormitory dining hall, all accompanied by the music of our favorite dance bands, including Glenn

Miller, Tommy Dorsey, and Benny Goodman, thanks to a modern record player—these are universal college experiences, although the music has changed. And, of course, there were great adventures. My roommate, Joan Hendry, and I got permission from her parents and my grandmother to sign up for the special "football train" when SMU was scheduled to play the University of Pittsburgh in the finals. Our school mascot, a small mustang horse named Peruna, occupied a special reserved stall in the baggage car and received student visitors throughout the two-day train trip from Dallas to Pittsburgh. As it turned out, Joan and I were among a small number of young women who had been able to get permission and financing for the trip. We stayed in the Tri Delta house on campus, and the house telephone rang nonstop with calls from young men wanting to escort us to events. Our Tri Delta sisters were mightily impressed, and we never explained to them that the ratio of available women to men on our "football special weekend" was strictly in our favor.

During my junior year, I became active in the campus YMCA/YWCA organization, and for the following summer, in 1941, I applied for a summer job in Estes Park, Colorado, at the beautiful YWCA conference grounds. The job combined interesting seminars, some work experience, and magnificent scenery. In the evenings the staff and college students would gather around a fire, where we had serious discussions about issues of the day, including race relations and Christian values. Since the staff included representatives from several historically black colleges, those of us from colleges that were predominantly white at the time had an opportunity to hear and better understand the concerns and obstacles our African American counterparts faced.

For our work duties, men were assigned as handymen, garbage collectors, and other positions, and women were either waitresses or housekeepers. We took advantage of our free time to enjoy and explore the beauty of Colorado's Rocky Mountains, including visits to Pikes Peak. I enjoyed the seminars and discussions at the conference center and dates with young men on the staff, but everything that happened that summer was eclipsed by my meeting a young man who was destined to become my husband, the father of my children, and my lifetime love.

One morning during my waitress break between breakfast and lunch, I strolled over to the post office to see if I had any mail. I had just picked up some letters when a young man walked in. I turned to glance at him, and as we made eye contact, I felt something I

From the moment I saw Sidney Earl Cockrell Jr.
in a crowded post office, I was smitten.

had never experienced before. We did not speak, but I must have been clearly smitten, because I walked back to my room somewhat in a daze and said to my roommate, "I think I have just met the man I am going to marry." She looked at me with great skepticism. I didn't even know his name. I didn't know anything about him. And yet somehow I just knew.

That day at lunch as I was serving my tables, a friend walked over and said, "There's a young man at my table who would like to have a date with you." Even before I turned my head to see who my friend was referring to, I knew who it would be.

Sidney Earl Cockrell Jr. was the boys' work secretary in the Tulsa, Oklahoma, YMCA. A graduate of the University of Oklahoma, Sid had been president of that campus's YMCA and had been active in many other college activities. He also held a reserve commission as a second lieutenant in the U.S. Army Reserve, having participated in ROTC at the university. In Estes Park for a YMCA boys' work secretaries conference, he would be there the rest of the week. We had a date every night, and we both felt by the end of the week that there was something special between us. Sid went home to Tulsa after his conference ended, and I hoped this was not just a summer romance that would fade away.

When my duties in Estes Park were over, I headed back to Fort Worth and stayed briefly with my grandmother before returning to Dallas in September to begin my senior year at SMU. That same month, Sid was called to active duty in the U.S. Army and

assigned to the 70th Field Artillery Battalion at Fort
Sill. The war in Europe was escalating, and America
wanted to be prepared to send troops if needed.

Sid visited Dallas as often as he could, driving the
nearly 200 miles from Fort Sill, and our romance
continued to thrive. I was working hard at winding
up my scholastic requirements and looking forward
to graduation in June. My senior year was a glorious time that included my selection as queen of the
theology school and a nomination for homecoming
queen. We rode in open convertibles in the homecoming parade, holding sprays of chrysanthemums,
and were presented to the crowds attending that
weekend's football game.

I was busy on the Student Council of Religious
Activities and in the campus YMCA/YWCA, and I
was elected chair of the North Texas Area Council of
Student Christian Associations, which also included
representatives of several black colleges. Discussions
similar to those I'd experienced in Estes Park convinced me that changes were badly needed in race
relations in the 1940s, and I hoped this organization
was an early starting point.

One of my favorite activities was participating
on the SMU debate team, traveling to out-of-town
competitions, learning the art of presenting and

defending a variety of ideas, and winning awards, including the coveted Mustang Award for outstanding service to the university. I also leapt at opportunities for extemporaneous speaking and radio narration; all these experiences proved invaluable in my later career in public life.

My senior year seemed to speed by, and as the end of the fall semester approached, I attended a YWCA weekend retreat in Glen Rose, Texas. The featured speaker was Dr. Sherwood Eddy, who shared his view that despite the war overseas, the Japanese would never attack the United States. That Sunday—December 7, 1941—he was proven wrong when Pearl Harbor was bombed and our country officially became a part of World War II. As we drove back to Dallas that Sunday afternoon, we knew our world had changed. From that moment through my graduation in the spring, life was much more serious.

In January 1942 I celebrated my twentieth birthday and the start of my last semester at SMU. The dark cloud of war was evident at the university, as many of the young men there were debating with themselves and their families about whether to leave school to enlist in the armed forces. I was deep into final coursework and papers, focusing on completing the requirements for graduation.

At my grandmother's recommendation, I had taken quite a few education courses. She knew that earning a permanent teacher's certificate in Texas would ensure that I would earn a living after graduation and explained that teaching was a fine choice of vocation for women. I followed my grandmother's advice, recognizing that there were few vocations open to women at that time. I recall that there was only one woman in my senior class enrolled in SMU's School of Engineering! Other careers open to women at the time were nursing, secretarial and office work, and retail sales. In the 1940s most young women married and became full-time homemakers.

As I pursued my teaching certificate, I undertook a research project for a senior-level education course examining how the concept of separate but equal education was working in the Dallas public school system. My study revealed that overall spending in the segregated schools for black children was about one-half the per capita spending in schools for white children. Salaries for black teachers were half of what their white counterparts with the same level of college training earned. The bottom line was that only the *separate* portion of the "separate but equal" mandate was being carried out. What was true for Dallas schools was probably also true for other school

districts in the state. It took the civil rights movement to effect change. I hoped to be a small part of
that change when I graduated that spring, prepared
to seek a teaching position in one of the state's public
school systems.

A surprise visit from Sid in April changed my
plans, however. He met me at my grandmother's
apartment, and we went to a drive-in theater to see
the movie *Brother Orchid*. With the sound system
attached to the open window of our car, we were
lined up next to other cars to watch the feature under
the stars, munching on popcorn delivered by roving
attendants. Not long into the movie, Sid proposed.
I don't remember one thing about that movie. I was
somewhat in a daze, and thrilled, and I accepted on
the spot. We talked about having a June wedding
following my graduation and continued talking
and talking until the show was over. Then we went
back to the apartment to share our plans with my
grandmother, who was pleased. Next we called my
parents, who had relocated to Kansas City, Missouri,
where Dad was serving as attorney-in-charge of the
district office of the Treasury Department's alcohol
tax unit. They had not yet met Sid, and they were
somewhat startled by our news. They immediately
made arrangements to come to Texas to meet my
fiancé, and our plans proceeded.

Sid and I were married in Fort Worth,
Texas, in 1942.

Our wedding took place three weeks after my
graduation from SMU. The ceremony was at the
First Methodist Church in Fort Worth on Saturday
evening, June 20, 1942, with Dr. J. N. R. Score, pastor
of the church, officiating. My roommate, Joan, was
maid of honor, and five of my closest friends at SMU

were bridesmaids. Sid's brother, Coleman G. (Tracy) Cockrell, was best man, and his groomsmen were his best friends, both military and civilian. I wore a white organdy wedding dress, and the bridesmaids wore yellow organdy gowns with ruffled skirts. Sid was so handsome in his white dress uniform, and my heart soared at the prospect of spending the rest of my life with him.

We spent our wedding night at the elegant Warwick Melrose Hotel in Dallas. The next day we drove to Siloam Springs in Arkansas, a popular honeymoon spot in the 1940s, known for its healing waters. I was so exhausted from the pressures of graduation and all of the prenuptial activities that I slept most of the way while Sid drove. When I woke up, I saw the Ozark Mountains in the distance and beautiful blooming dogwood trees surrounding the resort. After our week-long honeymoon, we drove to Fort Sill, in Lawton, Oklahoma, where we moved into a garage efficiency apartment Sid had found and rented for us. Housing was extremely tight in Lawton because of the wartime expansion of Fort Sill, so we felt fortunate to find our tiny love nest. I had left family, college, and old friends behind, and I was ready to begin a new phase in my life.

FOUR

Wife, Ensign, and Mother

1943–50

Lawton, Oklahoma, was known for its tornadoes. Our landlords showed us not only our new garage apartment but also the backyard storm cellar, advising that we had access to it in case of a storm warning. Over the course of the year, we received several late-night telephone calls urging us to hurry to the storm cellar to wait out the impending weather. We would hastily get up, don our bathrobes, and trot down the stairs to the cellar in the backyard. We would sit there for several hours, tuned in to a small transistor radio, until the warning was over. There were no direct tornado hits while we were in Lawton, but I'll never forget feeling like Dorothy in *The Wizard of Oz*, with the wind howling as we raced for that underground shelter.

As a bride, according to protocol, I was welcomed to the role of military wife by the 70th Field Artil-

Our life as a "military couple" began at Fort Sill, in Lawton, Oklahoma.

lery battalion commander, Maj. Louis Cantrell, and his wife. As I met the other officers and wives, I quickly came to understand that the rank of the officer also carried over to his wife. There was definitely a pecking order to military social life, and if the commander's wife did not like an officer's wife, promotions could be affected. While we enjoyed getting to know Sid's military associates, I felt more at home with friends we made through our church, the First Methodist Church of Lawton. The pastor was the Rev. Herbert Cockerill, and the similarity of our names made our welcome there even warmer. I soon became the church's director of youth activities, a position I really enjoyed.

One of our best military friends was Lt. Anson Ivan Dreisen, who had been one of Sid's groomsmen. He had a great sense of humor and was fond of remarking how challenging it would have been if he'd joined the navy. He would have been called Ensign Anson Ivan Dreisen; saying it aloud made us all laugh uproariously.

Sid's parents, Edna and Sid Cockrell Sr., often drove over from their home in Tulsa to visit. In her youth, Mom Cockrell had been dubbed the Voice of Oklahoma when she was the featured singer on a radio program, and she had a beautiful soprano voice. She was also a wonderful cook and an avid bridge player. She knew the Goren bridge book rules by heart and often played in duplicate bridge tournaments. Dad Cockrell, on the other hand, did not play by the rule book, and a combination of natural instincts and good luck often made him the winner, much to Mom Cockrell's annoyance. He was a retired printer, who enjoyed gardening on their little farm. His stories about the early days of automobile ownership were immensely entertaining.

According to Mom Cockrell, in the mid-1920s Sid and his brother, Coleman, would stretch out on the wide running boards of the family's touring sedan, equipped with soft pillows, to enjoy the breeze as the car slowly bumped along the dirt roads on summer days. Because of those early roads in Oklahoma, they stopped every few miles to change flat tires. The drive from Tulsa to Lawton was much easier some twenty years later, and their visits were always wonderful occasions.

The first year of marriage sped by, and in spring 1943 I accepted a teaching position at a nearby elementary school after a teacher departed when her military husband was transferred. A short time later, the 70th Field Artillery Battalion was ordered to move to Fort Jackson in Columbia, South Carolina, and Sid left with his unit in May. I stayed in Lawton to finish the school term and wrap up our affairs and joined him in June. Housing in Columbia was scarce, so we shared a two-bedroom house with another young officer and his wife, Lt. and Mrs. Robert Boroff. Each couple had a bedroom and bath, and we shared the kitchen facilities.

Temperatures soared to over 100 degrees in Columbia in the summer. As Sid's battalion was ordered on field marches in the hot sun, we were guessing that the 70th would receive orders to go to North Africa and that the troops were being prepared for desert warfare. Their secret orders arrived in July. The parting was painful for the wives as we thought of our husbands going off to a battle zone. After lots of hugs and kisses, and some tears, I said good-bye to Sid and headed to Kansas City, where my parents had a welcoming place for me in their comfortable and spacious home.

Imagine my surprise when Sid's first V-mail arrived for me in Kansas City, letting me know that the 70th had been sent to Boston, where they had been issued arctic gear, and then they had boarded a troopship and sailed for Iceland. The battalion had been placed on a relatively fast former passenger liner converted to a troopship for wartime service; they had evaded an enemy submarine attack during their voyage across the Atlantic Ocean and arrived safely in Iceland, one of the staging and mobilization areas that would later launch the Allied forces' major offensive in Europe. Over time I received many more Victory Mail messages from Sid—miniature, microfilmed communiqués that were used to expedite mail during the war—but knowing he was in snow rather than sand was a happy shock.

Stationed in Iceland in 1943, Sid (*right*) served as aide-de-camp for Maj. Gen. William S. Key (*center*).

The base in Iceland was under the command of Maj. Gen. William S. Key, who was a National Guard general from Oklahoma. A few months after Sid's arrival in Iceland, he was contacted by General Key's aide-de-camp, who advised Sid that he was under consideration for an appointment as General Key's new aide. It was General Key's custom to select a young officer from Oklahoma to serve in that capacity whenever his current aide was promoted to another assignment. After an interview with the general, Sid received the appointment and was detached from the 70th, which later went on to fight in the Battle of the Bulge, where many casualties were reported.

Meanwhile, back in Kansas City, I put in my application for officer training with the WAVES, the women's reserve organization for the navy. Knowing Sid would probably be overseas for the duration of the war, I wanted to do my part. I had first thought I would volunteer for the American Red Cross and that I might qualify as a recreational service officer with overseas duty. The minimum age for Red Cross duty, however, was twenty-five, and I was only twenty-one. I decided to apply to the Department of the Navy for the WAVES officer candidate school; my orders arrived in August 1943. I boarded a train for Northampton, Massachusetts, where the WAVES were lodged in a converted hotel, and I entered the program as an apprentice seaman. Our academic classes were held on the campus of Smith College, and we marched from the hotel to our classes in formation, learning to call out military marching commands as we went up and down the hills of Northampton.

All the classes were about the navy—naval ships and aircraft identification, naval history, naval customs, naval personnel, naval law, and other subjects that were completely new to us. Not surprisingly, with the deluge of information, and all the marching up and down the hills, we were exhausted by the end of each day and glad to return to our living quarters at the hotel.

Four women were assigned to each room, with double-decker bunks, and a shared bath. Meal service in the hotel dining room was served cafeteria-style on trays, and the food was good. On the whole, morale was high; the only time we were sad was when we learned that one of our comrades had flunked out of the rigorous training program and had to return home. I felt especially sorry for another recruit from Kansas City, who had resigned from a very good position as an executive secretary to the president of one of the major banks to become a WAVE. She had been given a huge send-off at the railroad station by a host of well-wishers. She was a very smart woman and had passed all the academic requirements, but she had difficulty with the marching and calling out the military commands in proper cadence. I know it must have been very embarrassing for her to have to return home to Kansas City, and I was glad that only my parents had accompanied me to the railroad station, knowing that I could slip quietly home if my candidacy met a similar fate.

Fortunately, I passed all the academic tests and discovered that I really liked the marching, calling out those commands, and singing along the way. The official WAVES song was "WAVES of the Navy," sung in counterpoint to "Anchors Aweigh." Recalling my mother's story about the patriotic concert she attended just prior to my birth, I have always felt my love of marching bands started in the womb. After passing about four weeks of training courses, I became a midshipman; upon graduation a few weeks later, I received my commission as an ensign. My orders arrived in November; I learned that I had been assigned to the Bureau of Ships, in Washington, DC.

Our group was sent to a temporary housing complex for the WAVES when we arrived, which gave us time to familiarize ourselves with Washington and to find affordable housing. After checking in at the personnel office in the Navy Department's Bureau of Ships, I learned that I had been assigned to the personnel office in the position of education officer. This meant I would be in charge of administering all of the ratings advancement tests for enlisted personnel in the bureau. Additionally, for military drill

With Sid stationed overseas, I joined the
war effort as well and became an ensign
in the WAVES.

purposes I would serve as a company commander in
the Bureau of Ships Regiment of WAVES.

I settled into my responsibilities and began learning
the procedures for administering the ratings advance-

ment tests. As it turned out, it was not very exciting.
The two principal ratings for enlisted personnel in
our bureau were yeoman and storekeeper; we gave
tests about once a month to thirty or forty women
on a given day. The tests had to be individually read
and graded, and the process was time-consuming
and rather tedious. Looking back, I realize what a
world of difference computers, which would not
be invented for several decades, would have made.
I also served as a counselor for enlisted personnel
who were trying to complete degree requirements
by correspondence with colleges or universities, and
that was more interesting. But what I liked best were
my additional duties as a company commander for
military drills and reviews. Even today, at ninety-six
years old, when I hear "The Stars and Stripes Forever," I am ready to march. I was learning that career
building often means a combination of somewhat
dull tasks and tasks that are inspiring and fulfilling.

Through friends I met as a new member of the
congregation at the Mount Vernon Place Methodist
Church, I learned about an efficiency apartment that
would soon be available. It was in a building located
at 921 K Street NW, within walking distance of the
Navy Department. Another WAVE agreed to be my
roommate, and we were happy to move out of the

barracks-like quarters into a more pleasant, homelike environment.

Mary Griffith was from Denver, Colorado, where she had been an attorney in a law firm with her two older brothers when she volunteered for active duty. A little older than I was, Mary applied for—and received—a direct commission as a lieutenant, junior grade, in the WAVES, one rank above ensign. She came from a patriotic family of strong Democrats, and with Roosevelt in the White House, she was invited to many events in Washington, DC. My family background was Republican, so having Mary as a roommate gave me an important opportunity to gain some insights into how political parties differed in philosophy and positions on issues. Washington, DC, in the mid-1940s was the hub of the wartime universe for the United States and its allies, and it offered young women like Mary and me a glimpse into the much bigger world.

The Bureau of Ships personnel office was handling many of the details for a gala performance benefitting navy widows and orphans in a downtown theater, and I had purchased three general admission tickets. I invited Mary and another friend, Eileen Burdick, whose father was Congressman Usher Burdick of North Dakota, to be my guests. A day or two before the performance, a new recruit had joined the Bureau of Ships through my office, and she quickly volunteered to serve as an usher for the upcoming event. That night brought rain; cabs were impossible to find, and my guests and I arrived at the theater as the lights dimmed for the program to start. We were greeted enthusiastically by our newest recruit, who said, "Follow me, Ensign Cockrell. I know just where there are three good seats." Ushering us down the dark aisle, she led us closer and closer to the stage and finally pointed to three seats on the aisle. As we sank down into the seats, I glanced to my right. All I could see was gold braid. Our young neophyte seaman had placed us in the admirals' row! I realized I was sitting next to an admiral's wife, and I whispered, "I know we are in the wrong row." She whispered back, "You're in a very nice row, my dear, so just stay put."

The emcee came onstage, the lights came up, and he began to introduce the "distinguished guests in the front"—Rear Admiral Cochrane, chief of the Bureau of Ships, and Mrs. Cochrane, followed by the other admirals and their wives. Finally he got to me, gave me a hard look, and said, "And that concludes our distinguished guests." Years later when I was introduced as a distinguished guest at various events,

I always chuckled to myself, remembering that we all start in the general admission section.

Meanwhile Sid's career was blossoming. As the aide to General Key, the commanding general of the Iceland Base Command, he handled diverse diplomatic assignments, ranging from orchestrating the proper seating for the Russian ambassador and his wife, who spoke only Russian and French, to sailing to northern Iceland through a ferocious midwinter storm to review troops. He also accompanied the general when he met important Icelandic officials as that country prepared to celebrate its independence from Denmark. As a result of his connections, I was invited by Thor Thordarson, Iceland's ambassador to the United States, to attend a beautiful reception that he and his wife hosted in Washington. When Iceland was proclaimed an independent nation, it was an emotional and historic time in that country, of course, and also in Washington, which was not only the capital of our country but also the capital of the free world in those days.

The U.S. troops in Iceland had to adjust to cold, dark winters, with only four hours or so of daylight; the reverse was true in the summer, when it did not get dark until almost midnight. Keeping up morale was sometimes a problem, especially for troops stationed in more remote outposts such as weather stations. There were several suicides, which caused a great deal of concern within the command, reminding us all of the sacrifices soldiers make during wartime, far from home and sometimes far from the battlefield.

When spring 1944 arrived, I had a perfectly wonderful surprise. One evening when I got home from work, I received a telephone call from Sid. He and General Key were in Washington! They had arrived for high-level consultations at the Pentagon on issues affecting the Iceland Base Command. My roommate, Mary, graciously volunteered to stay with her friend, Eileen Burdick, so Sid could stay in the apartment with me. We had a joyous reunion.

Sid was busy accompanying the general during the day, of course, and I reported to work each day, but we could be together in the evening. I also took a few days of leave to accompany Sid and General Key on a trip to Boston, where they had appointments at the Boston Navy Yard regarding shipments to the Iceland Base Command. I decided to go separately to see the navy yard, and when I presented my ID badge, I received an especially cordial reception. An escort officer gave me a complete tour, as well as an extensive briefing on all of the recent activities, heavily weighted with "success stories." When I was finally able to take my leave, my escort's parting words were "Please be sure to give us a good report when you get back to the Bureau of Ships." The Boston Navy Yard had been expecting an official from the bureau, and I was mistaken for that person. I always wondered what the navy yard thought when a second officer from the bureau arrived that month.

Sid and General Key returned to Iceland, and I was left with wonderful memories of a very happy week. Preparations for a big springtime regimental parade and review of WAVES helped distract me from missing my husband, who was once again 3,000 miles away. This would be my opportunity as a company commander to make sure the women in my command performed well. We practiced and practiced, marching and executing military commands, and at the big review in spring 1944, we were named the Best Commanded and Performed Company of the WAVES in the Bureau of Ships Regiment of WAVES. Each woman received a certificate of commendation for our achievement; I have treasured mine for nearly seventy-five years.

I had assumed that my military career would extend for the duration of the war, but I learned that Mother Nature had other plans. After that wonderful reunion with Sid, I discovered that I was pregnant, and there was one little matter that I needed to take care of. I had not mentioned Sid's Washington visit to anyone back home, because he and General Key were on secret orders and I was following security requirements. As I wrote to my friends to tell them my joyous news, I had to let them know that Sid had been with me for that glorious reunion. In the middle of the summer, I accepted my honorable discharge from the WAVES and headed back to Kansas City to await the birth of our child.

Once again I made my home with my family, in the house they rented from Col. Per Ramee, who had served in World War I and had just retired. His wife had recently died, and he planned to move into his downtown club but wanted a responsible family to live in his home, furnished with beautiful things he and his wife had gathered during his military service all over the world. Mother took great care of the furnishings, polishing the silver serving pieces and brass samovars and enjoying the other objects that filled the lovely home. From time to time Colonel Ramee would come for dinner; he always exclaimed that the house had never looked lovelier. Several of the colonel's grown children were serving as officers in various branches of the military, and from time to time one would arrive to ask permission to retrieve

During World War II every American family
received food ration books for items like butter
and sugar that were in short supply.

some left-behind possession. Mother would chuckle
to herself as they headed down to the basement, where
she had discovered a stash of liquor. She had carefully
covered it, but she knew the stash decreased with each
sibling's visit. Mother also found packages of cigarettes
hidden in some of the draperies around the house.

Apparently Colonel and Mrs. Ramee had been strict parents, even when their children became adults.

During the war a number of items were rationed. Each family received ration books with stamps that had to accompany purchases of those rationed items. It took careful planning to have good meals and make the rationed items stretch. We had a little cocker spaniel named Blackie that interfered with this complicated process when he jumped on the breakfast table while Mother was occupied in the kitchen and gobbled up a quarter pound of highly rationed butter. At that time butter was considered a special treat, and little Blackie was certainly disgraced.

Mrs. Ramee had laid in a large supply of canned goods in the basement, especially canned fruits that were on the ration list. When Mother told Colonel Ramee that she had found this incredible bounty, he told her to use anything she found and not let it spoil. She used it to supplement our meals, and we felt like we had discovered buried treasure in that basement.

Most of my friends in Kansas City were war brides as I was, awaiting their babies at home with their parents. We would get together to play cards, exchange news gleaned from our husbands' letters, and, of course, discuss our pregnancies. That fall I felt fortunate to be in my family's welcoming home

Carol Ann Cockrell
was born on
January 25, 1945,
the happy result of
Sid's classified visit
to Washington nine
months earlier.

while I waited for the baby. Based on the sound of the heartbeat, my obstetrician had predicted that the baby would be a boy, and we had decided to name him Robert Bruce Cockrell, to carry on the Robert Bruce part of my father's name. When the baby arrived on January 25, 1945, however, we were the parents of a beautiful baby girl. Sid had applied for leave to come home from Iceland, but the baby arrived a little early, and he arrived a few days later. After a quick consultation, Baby Girl Cockrell became Carol Ann Cockrell.

Sid stayed for about three weeks, getting acquainted with Carol Ann, before returning to Iceland, where he was now Major Cockrell, having been promoted from aide to base commandant to captain and then major in time for it to be printed on Carol Ann's birth announcement.

That spring it was clear that the war in Europe was winding down. On May 9, 1945, V–E Day became a reality with the signing of the peace treaty in Reims, France. Everyone in our country celebrated. The newspapers were full of people hugging each other, dancing, and giving thanks that the war in Europe had ended. A few months later, on September 2, the war with Japan came to a close with V–J Day. World War II was over! The men and women in the armed forces began to be deployed home. Sid was offered the opportunity to apply for regular army status and continue in military service, but he chose to keep his reserve status and return to civilian life. A new chapter as a husband and father was beginning.

With Sid's return, we set out on the first of several moves we would make over the next ten years, each necessitated by the various positions that Sid held in civilian life. First we gathered up our baby and belongings, much like my great-grandparents had done with little Julia more than fifty years before, and drove to Tulsa in our black Pontiac coupe with a rumble seat, which we bought used for $700. Sid had accepted his former position as boys' work secretary for the YMCA, and we used our $5,000 nest egg, accumulated during the war, to buy our first home, a colonial cottage with white columns in front. My grandmother Julia was so pleased with our thrift that she made a gift to us of a matching amount, so we paid in cash the full $10,000 for the house. We acquired hand-me-down furniture that my parents weren't using since their house in Kansas City was furnished, so we were all set for our new life.

Mom and Dad Cockrell lived in Tulsa too, and they were completely captivated by their granddaughter, nicknaming her Sugar Pie. Because there had been so many boys in the extended Cockrell family, a girl was an especially welcome addition. We joined the Presbyterian church Sid had attended before the war and renewed some of his old friendships. I reconnected with Betty Ann Tongue, my sorority sister from SMU, who had married Murray Rickman. Our circle of friends grew, and life in Tulsa was idyllic.

But just six months later Sid was invited to apply for the position of executive director of the Kentucky chapter of the National Conference of Christians and Jews (NCCJ), in Louisville. Realizing that his boss at the YMCA was not likely to retire for many years, Sid saw greater opportunity in Louisville, went for the interview, and was hired.

As it turned out, Mom Cockrell had relatives there, and they welcomed us warmly when we arrived. The Vick family helped us search for a new house, offering advice about neighborhoods, and we purchased a small two-story home in the St. Matthews suburb. Sid's organization had a wonderful board of directors, and he enjoyed his new position. The NCCJ, headquartered in New York with chapters throughout the country, was dedicated to promoting friendship and understanding between Christians and Jews, trying to overcome intolerance and prejudice. With Sid's own deep faith and inherent respect for others, and his skill as a public speaker, he was a good choice for the position and soon was in demand at luncheons and other events.

While I enjoyed being a homemaker and the mother of a toddler, I soon felt the need for some outside activity. I had read some interesting articles in the newspapers about the League of Women Voters, an organization that would become my passion for many years. When I met someone who belonged, I asked her if it was an invitational organization, thinking it might be like the Junior League. She laughed and told me anyone could join and that it was a nonpartisan organization that selected issues to study but did not endorse candidates for election. Then, if consensus was reached, the league took a position on the issue. At the time I joined, the Louisville league had taken the position to support a new state constitution for Kentucky. I began to study the issue and became so well briefed on it that I was asked to represent the league at speaking engagements in the community. Eventually I was asked to represent it during a televised debate. My colleague on the pro side of the debate was the state's attorney general, and two prominent lawyers represented the con side. When the debate was over—our side won—quite a few listeners complimented me on how well informed I was about the issues. I smiled and thanked them, secretly relieved that no one had asked me how long I had lived in Kentucky. A few years later, while I was president of the League of Women Voters in Dallas, we debated a new state constitution for Texas, and my experience in Kentucky had prepared me well.

Sid did such a good job in his position that he was

By 1924 the League of Women Voters, established by Carrie Chapman Catt in 1920, had chapters in 346 locations. I joined two decades later in Kansas City and later served as chapter president when we lived in Dallas.

noticed by the national president of the NCCJ, Dr. Everett R. Clinchy, who asked him to become the assistant to the president and to relocate to New York City. I was always deeply in love with my husband, and every time he got a promotion, I was happy. I never minded moving for his career. We packed our belongings and headed to New York City.

We moved into a fourth-floor walk-up on the East Side, in the 60s, just off Lexington Avenue. The location was nice, but the four flights of stairs were a challenge, especially when carrying groceries and a toddler. We were delighted when we found a wonderful apartment on Riverside Drive overlooking the Hudson River, where I had been taken for walks and treated to boxes of raisins as a little girl. The apartment was on the fifth floor, with a beautiful view, and best of all, the building had an elevator. My cousin John Banks, from San Antonio, was in New York completing his master's degree at Columbia University, and he volunteered to babysit Carol Ann when we wanted a night out. In appreciation, I always prepared a tasty home-cooked meal for him to share with us before Sid and I went out the door, usually for a show at a nearby movie theater.

Our sojourn in New York lasted about a year. Sid felt honored to have worked with Dr. Clinchy, for whom he had tremendous respect, but we missed being closer to family and friends. When Sid learned that the regional director of the NCCJ in Dallas, Hastings Harrison, was looking for a replacement for his top assistant, Sid asked Dr. Clinchy for permission to apply. Permission was granted, and Sid was promptly hired. We were going back to Texas!

FIVE

Back to Texas

1948–55

Dallas was a booming city of more than 400,000 people when we moved there in 1948. The Mercantile National Bank Building, with thirty-one floors, was the city's tallest skyscraper, and the historic Adolphus Hotel was still the most elegant hotel in town. The Cotton Bowl Stadium, home to the state fair and college football games, had just added a deck, increasing its capacity to 67,000 to accommodate the fans who flocked to watch the famous halfback Doak Walker, who had played for my alma mater.

We purchased an attractive home on Horseshoe Trail, in a new housing area where many families with young children lived. On July 12, 1948, Sid and I welcomed the birth of our second daughter, Cathy Lynn Cockrell, who immediately became Sweetie Pie to Mom and Dad Cockrell.

Moving back to Dallas gave me the chance to

We moved to Dallas, Texas, in 1948, and baby Cathy's
birth there made us a family of four.

reconnect with old friends from my college days and with the organization I had so enjoyed in Louisville—the League of Women Voters. Dorothy Ruggles was its president, and she was a well-organized, articulate leader during a time when the organization addressed some of the most important governmental issues of the day. Her husband, William B. Ruggles, was the editor of the *Dallas Morning News* editorial page and a powerful sounding board for the organization. I immediately volunteered to organize a younger women's discussion group at our home, and soon there were twenty-five of us, all in our mid-to-late twenties, and all young mothers. We shared the expense of hiring a babysitter who watched our toddlers as they played in the fenced backyard while we discussed important issues in the living room.

A meeting in the fall attracted all twenty-five members, along with twenty-five young children. I was concentrating on conducting the meeting and harboring some concern about whether the sitter could handle that many children outside, and I had a lapse of memory that added a lot of excitement to the day.

Baby Cathy had developed an allergy to her formula, so her doctor had prescribed a complicated process for preparing the formula. I had to boil a can of evaporated milk for an hour, then let it cool to lukewarm before putting it in her bottle. I had started the process shortly before my guests arrived, and I became engrossed in the discussion under way at the meeting. Suddenly there was an explosion in my kitchen. It sounded like a bomb had gone off. I rushed in to find that the pot had boiled dry, the can of milk had exploded, and caramelized milk had covered the ceiling, walls, and floor. I turned off the stove, closed the door, and returned to finish the discussion. After the meeting was over, I surveyed that dismal scene. The milk had hardened into something resembling shellac, and it took me weeks to get the kitchen completely cleaned. Despite the kitchen fiasco we had a great meeting, with discussions ranging from establishing family courts for the Texas judicial system, to improved legal rights for women. All in all, it was a wonderful day!

Our family joined the congregation of the Westminster Presbyterian Church, and we developed deep friendships there. I was elected president of the young adult Sunday school class, which was taught by our pastor, the Rev. Anton J. Van Pufelin. Sid was an elected elder and served on the session, comprised of ruling elders of the church. Carol took piano lessons there and participated in recitals in the fellowship hall. A large part of our family life was centered in our church, and we were saddened by a dispute that ripped the congregation apart and led to the departure of our beloved pastor, who had been a proponent of change. Many younger members of the church, particularly young families with children, wanted to expand services to include a Christian day school and day care center. The session, comprised mostly of older members, denied the request and the pastor resigned. A number of the families left Westminster Presbyterian and became founding members of the Northwest Presbyterian Church, where a building program was started; the new church grew and became an important part of our lives.

Our alma maters were also an important part of our lives in those days. Sid was an active alumnus of the University of Oklahoma and president of the Dallas OU Club. The rivalry between Oklahoma and the University of Texas always reached its peak when their annual football game was played in the famous Cotton Bowl. The night before the game, the two alumni groups would hold parties, one at the Baker Hotel, and the other at the Adolphus. The two hotels were across the street from each other, and as the evening wore on, a skirmish or two often took place on the street.

One year when Oklahoma was invited to play in the Sugar Bowl, the Dallas OU Club chartered a football train equipped with Pullman sleeping cars for the trip to New Orleans. The train stayed in the New Orleans railroad station for a couple of nights and served as our hotel during our stay. The food was so delicious on the diner that many fans making the trip never bothered to sample the renowned New Orleans cuisine. We did not want to miss that gourmet opportunity, however, and enjoyed incredible meals at Antoine's, Galatoire's, and the Commander's Palace.

Annual Fourth of July parties at the home of Joyce and Gene Mohr, both friends from SMU days, were a highlight of those years in Dallas, reminiscent of the celebrations I remembered as a child. Barbecue and fireworks, children playing happily, and my favorite patriotic music combined to create unforgettable evenings that reminded us of everything good about this wonderful country.

Country and community have always been important to me, and I became even more involved with the League of Women Voters when I was elected to its board. I served first as its public relations chair, organizing a major event at the Dallas fairgrounds with state attorney general John Ben Shepherd as the featured speaker. I also served as chair of the residential campaign for the American Red Cross and as vice president of the newly organized United Nations Society. The president of that organization was Sarah T. Hughes, who later administered the oath of office as president of the United States to Lyndon B. Johnson, following the assassination of President John F. Kennedy. All of these civic roles were challenging and interesting, and they definitely broadened my horizons.

In 1951 we bought a new home on Douglas Street in the Preston Hollow neighborhood. Carol was enrolled in first grade at Preston Hollow Elementary School, and I became active in the PTA. Soon I became aware of various organizations that were gathering steam as the McCarthyism movement grew. One group was called the Minute Women, and another was the Facts Forum, and while they were supported by many persons motivated by feelings of patriotism, they raised suspicion and apprehension in the community and focused on generating distrust of many organizations and individuals.

One day at a PTA meeting I was surprised when a spokesperson for the Minute Women submitted a resolution opposing the United Nations Education, Scientific, and Cultural Organization (UNESCO).

She gave a speech condemning the organization, labeling it anti-American, and urged support of the resolution to oppose it. She called for an immediate vote on the issue by the PTA membership. Our local PTA had never taken a position on national or international issues before, but it appeared that this one was headed for a vote. I felt that our PTA, whose members had worked together in goodwill on so many projects and issues supporting our children and their school, was being pushed into taking a position on an issue that most members were not familiar with. I pointed out that we had only heard one side of a controversial issue and recommended that we hear both sides before a vote was taken. After some discussion the membership agreed. When the meeting was over, I was contacted by the PTA president to come to a planning meeting to arrange for a panel presentation on the issue. We decided to hold it in the evening to permit a large number of people to attend.

The selection of the moderator was also discussed at the planning meeting. The woman representing those opposing UNESCO suggested that Dan Smoot, executive director of Facts Forum, serve as the moderator. I responded that I did not think he would be appropriate in the role since his organization had

Family time was always the most important part of my life, and I loved watching Cathy (*left*) and Carol (*right*) grow up.

been publicly identified as having a position already. The woman who recommended him was outraged at my opposition. I reiterated that it was important to have an impartial moderator agreeable to all parties. I suggested the name of a well-respected bank official who was known to be a conservative and therefore might be acceptable to the Minute Women but who would also be fair and impartial. My suggestion was accepted, and planning proceeded.

The event attracted widespread attention and a large audience. It was covered in the local press, as well as in national print media, including the *Christian Science Monitor.* I felt that speakers on both sides presented their views effectively. In the end, the PTA decided not to pass any resolution regarding UNESCO. This incident reinforced my belief in the value of being willing to stand up for what you feel is important, even if you feel you might be in the minority position or it involves risk.

After living in Preston Hollow for a few years, we received an attractive offer for the property and decided to accept. Our daughters were growing, and we looked for a home in Highland Park because the school district was considered the best in the state. After some serious house hunting, we purchased an older English Tudor–style home. The house had a basement, which was unusual since most homes there had slab foundations. When we explored it, we discovered that the house had a notorious past. During Prohibition it was the site of the neighborhood still, producing spirits for a host of parties. We found thank-you notes for "favors" that had reportedly enhanced the good times at various events, ranging from debutante parties to men's bachelor parties and a myriad of other happenings. I thought about my grandfather and his work during Prohibition and wondered what he would think.

~

The girls were doing well. Carol Ann was in third grade at Bradfield School, and Cathy was starting first grade. They were making friends in the neighborhood, and Cathy's "best friend" was the daughter of one of my SMU friends who had been a homecoming cheerleader with me during our brief moment of glory. Nine-year-old Carol was continuing to show musical talent. Our happy home even included two pet cats, Blackie and Goldie. Sid accepted a position as the assistant executive director of the Better Business Bureau, welcoming the opportunity to work more closely with the Dallas business community, and I was serving as the president of the League of Women Voters. We had definitely settled in.

Then, in 1955, Sid learned that friends had recommended him for the position of executive director of the Bexar County Medical Society in San Antonio. He agreed to an interview and asked me to accompany him, knowing I would enjoy seeing my Banks family relatives. Mom and Dad Cockrell agreed to stay in our home and look after the girls and the cats while we made the trip. We were off to see what the future might hold in San Antonio.

Falling in Love with a River

1955–63

On a beautiful autumn day we joined my uncle, Stanley Banks, for lunch at the Original Mexican Restaurant in downtown San Antonio. After our meal Uncle Stanley led us down a stairway to a sidewalk along the San Antonio River, which runs through the city. As we walked along that pathway, I became completely enchanted. A lush, tropical landscape surrounded us, a sharp contrast to the busy life at street level, and beautiful old stone pedestrian bridges crossed the river along the way. Mariachi music floated through the air from one of the colorful restaurants above. If it is possible to fall in love with a river, that's what happened on that November day in 1955.

The Bexar County Medical Society was housed in an elegant old mansion in the Monte Vista neighborhood that had once belonged to the Bedell Moore

The moment I saw the beautiful San Antonio River, I fell in love with the Alamo City.

family. Sid was interviewed by a selection committee, comprised of doctors who held leadership roles at the society, including Dr. Bob Gossett, Dr. John R. Smith, Dr. Jack Partain, and Dr. John Matthews. Sid came away from the meeting feeling optimistic, and I remember saying, "Now if they offer you this position, please accept. I love this place." Not long after we got home that evening, the telephone rang.

Sid was offered the position and accepted. That special feeling I experienced on the San Antonio River has lasted more than sixty-five years.

Moving is always a chore, and this would be our tenth move in just ten years. We put our Dallas house on the market and wrapped up our commitments, and Sid reported to his new office in early January. I stayed behind so the girls could complete the semester at Bradfield School, and in mid-January we joined Sid in San Antonio, where he had rented a house that proved way too small for all our belongings. We were motivated house hunters and quickly found a house in the Jefferson neighborhood where Uncle Stanley and Aunt Annie lived. It had a large living room with a fireplace, a spacious dining room, three bedrooms, and one bath. There was a lovely front porch overlooking a yard with two date palm trees. The backyard had five producing pecan trees, which reminded me of my grandmother and my former pecan-shelling duties at Christmastime. Carol entered fifth grade and Cathy entered second grade at nearby Woodlawn Elementary School.

We spent our first Sunday morning in San Antonio as new members of Grace Presbyterian Church. Later that day we received a call from Dr. and Mrs. L. Bonham Jones on behalf of the church. During the course of the conversation, I learned that Mrs. Jones's first name was Velma, and with that information I knew we were destined to become great friends. The other Velma Jones in my life was my mother! The Joneses had four children—Bonnie, who was Carol's age, Leana, Glenda, who was Cathy's age, and Justin.

~

Once again our church became an important part of our lives, and we embraced the wonderful fellowship there. Sid was again elected a deacon, and we both were asked to take over as the teachers of the adult Sunday school class. A number of civic leaders, including Mayor Ed Kuykendall and his wife, were part of the class, and on Wednesday evenings we all gathered at the church for a covered-dish supper. Sid and Carol joined the choir, and both girls participated in a variety of church programs. I remember one Christmas pageant in particular. Three young brothers cast as the wise men were standing at the back of the church, ready for their cue to come down the aisle bearing their gifts. Somehow they became confused and were halfway down the aisle when they realized they were ahead of schedule. In unison, they reversed direction, got down on their hands and knees, and crawled along the aisle to the back of the church. The pageant continued as we tried to contain our laughter.

Velma and Bonham Jones became our best friends, and in 1957 we bought adjacent cottages at Lake McQueeney, where we spent wonderful weekends. Our cottage had just one large room that included a living area, kitchen, and bathroom. Dad Cockrell volunteered to build a sleeping porch for the cottage, a true labor of love. He was an enthusiastic if not always accurate carpenter, and the completed porch always remained a little askew. We spent many a happy night on that handmade porch, lulled to sleep by the gentle summer breezes. All of us, except for Bonham, learned to water-ski. Bonham was a general practitioner, and since his practice included surgery, he did not want to risk breaking an arm or sustaining an injury that would prevent him from operating.

∼

Days of water-skiing, swimming, and floating around the dock on inner tubes, followed by evenings with potluck suppers, games, jigsaw puzzles, or easy conversation among friends, created times our family would cherish forever. Mom and Dad Cockrell had moved to San Antonio to be near us, and sometimes Mom Cockrell would host marathon bridge games at the lake cottage during the week. Our Christmas letter that year, sent to family and friends, mentioned the cottage at the lake and reported that Carol, a seventh grader at Horace Mann Junior School, was making straight As and serving as president of her homeroom and had won the talent show with her medley of tunes played on her accordion. She also served on the Presbytery Youth Council. Cathy, a fourth grader, was active in the Brownies.

~

While our life in San Antonio centered on social and cultural activities similar to those we'd pursued in Dallas, I was excited to discover that my new hometown offered much more diversity than I'd ever known. There was a much larger Hispanic population, and everything from music and food to architecture and fashion were enhanced by San Antonio's Latino influences. I now had two favorite types of music—marching bands and mariachis!

Despite a vow to myself to spend more time at home, I found myself volunteering for many organizations that help maintain our society's fabric—educational, religious, and political. The PTA enabled us to influence important school issues, chaperoning at teen dances gave us important insights about our children and their developing social skills, church activities provided a crucial moral compass, and the League of Women Voters offered a way to stay abreast of critical issues in our community and beyond. Soon I found myself serving as the president of more than one of the organizations behind these endeavors and wondered what had happened to my resolution to stay home and mind my own business.

Soon after I accepted a two-year term as president of the League of Women Voters, I began working on an amendment to the state constitution providing for county home rule, which the league supported. It was proposed as a bracketed bill, based on those counties with the largest populations and limited to only those counties that desired the opportunity, but there was opposition from county officials throughout the state who did not want to change the current provisions. One of the Bexar County commissioners, Sam Jorrie, was an ardent advocate, but it was an uphill battle that we did not win. The league also took positions on issues affecting the council-manager form of city government, which had been approved by the voters in 1951, after decades of strong mayoral control. The league supported this new form of government, and I was pleased to learn that Uncle Stanley had been a member of the charter-writing commission that launched the change.

Sid was also taking on leadership roles in the community. At our church he served first as a deacon and was then elected an elder. He was an active member of the Alamo Kiwanis Club and always loved volunteering at the Noche del Rio productions sponsored each summer at the Arneson River Theatre. He also supported the western art show at the annual stock show and rodeo, the American Heart Association, and the Salvation Army, where he served as chair of the board at one time, all in addition to serving in his full-time position at the Bexar County Medical Society. We had both grown up in families that believed in giving back to their communities, with a gratitude for the blessings we enjoyed in life and a desire to make life better for people who were less fortunate. I think this attitude is timeless, just as valuable now as it was then.

Sid's work took him to annual American Medical Association meetings around the country, and we often combined our family vacations with those trips. His expenses, including airfare and lodging, were paid, but instead of going by plane, Sid would load us in the car, and off we would go to places like Miami, Chicago, San Francisco, and New York.

Once the meeting was over, we would embellish the trip with excursions to nearby points of interest. After the Miami meeting we stayed at a beachfront hotel, and the Bonham Jones family joined us; after the Chicago conference we headed to the Wisconsin Dells, visited Frank Lloyd Wright's masterpiece Fallingwater, and attended a Native American ceremony in an outdoor amphitheater.

One of the performers was an older Native American man who was talented in giving realistic bird and animal calls. During his performance, an unscheduled performer tried to get into the act. A Chihuahua dog popped out of a large tote bag in the possession of the woman sitting behind us. After each birdcall, the tiny dog responded with a loud resounding howl. Most of the audience found it amusing, but after receiving a baleful look from the performer, the dog's owner made a hasty retreat, taking her dog and tote bag with her.

Before the meeting in San Francisco, we drove to Los Angeles, with overnight stays along the way in New Mexico and Arizona, then enjoyed a leisurely drive up California's famous Pacific Coast Highway with a stop at San Simeon to see the incredible estate that once belonged to publishing magnate William Randolph Hearst. Following the New York conference, we visited Niagara Falls and were awed by that incredible force of nature. These family trips were wonderful experiences, not only because we saw interesting places together but also because long hours in the small space of our car ensured the kind of bonding that is more difficult in these days of increased airplane travel and so many electronic devices that distract from one-on-one conversation. Those special summer trips became even more enjoyable once we purchased a car with air conditioning in 1958.

~

The 1950s were a time of prosperity in the United States. It was easy to see what Winston Churchill, then former British prime minister, meant when he said, "America at this moment stands at the summit of the world." Our country was the world's strongest military power, its economy was booming, and the fruits of prosperity—suburban houses, new cars, and other consumer goods—were available to more people than ever before. Our little family was comfortable and doing well. Carol had become quite a musician, first on the piano, then on the accordion, and Cathy enjoyed dancing and was a natural leader, serving as president of the sixth-grade Sunday school class, the junior choir, and her Girl Scout troop. And, in 1959, we purchased a beautiful, large home on Mary Louise Drive across the street from Uncle Stanley and Aunt Annie. At one time it had belonged to Aunt Annie's parents and had a French Normandy design with a circular staircase with a balcony that overlooked the two-story living room. My cousin, John Banks, told me that when he and his brother, Stanley Jr., were growing up, they would put mattresses on the first floor beneath the balcony and jump down. Fortunately our daughters never tried that stunt.

There was a courtyard in front of the house with a little bridge over a moat, giving the property a castle-like appearance. When we purchased the house, the moat had been filled with dirt, and flowers had been planted there. We restored the original water feature and stocked it with a large population of goldfish, which soon began to disappear. One evening Carol was coming home from a party when she and her date spotted a raccoon fishing in the moat, and the mystery of the disappearing fish was solved.

∼

As idyllic as our lives were, the 1950s were also a decade of smoldering conflict. The nascent civil

rights movement and the crusade against commu-
nism at home and abroad exposed underlying divisions in American society. African Americans had
been fighting racial discrimination for centuries, and
I had wanted to see change for more than a decade.
In the landmark 1954 Brown v. Board of Education
case, the Supreme Court declared that "separate
educational facilities" for African American children were "inherently unequal," something I had
discovered firsthand when I conducted the research
project for my advanced education course at SMU.
Rosa Parks's famous arrest for refusing to give up her
seat to a white passenger on a bus in Montgomery,
Alabama, fueled the growing civil rights movement
in 1955.

As the decade came to an end, my mother wanted
to see more of that bigger world. For several years my
parents had been living in Omaha, Nebraska, where
Dad was serving as the regional attorney for the alcohol tax unit of the Treasury Department. When he
turned seventy in 1959, he faced mandatory retirement. Mother knew the transition was going to be
hard for him, so she hatched a plan for them to go
to Hawaii for several months. At first Dad resisted,
but he finally realized that Mother meant business.
She had made it clear that if he wanted to share her

company for the next few months, he needed to start packing. Reluctantly, Dad agreed to go. Through a mutual friend, Mother had learned that a young woman from Honolulu, who was planning a trip to the mainland for several months, wanted to lease her home to a responsible family. It was a perfect arrangement, and the lease was signed. The home was located in Makiki Heights, a lovely residential section in the hills overlooking downtown Honolulu. Dad, who had been so reluctant to go, soon was most enthusiastic.

When the time came for them to vacate that house, Seymore Terry, a Makiki Heights neighbor, told Mother that he was planning an extended trip around the world and that the house sitter he had hired had just bought a condominium and could not do the job. Mr. Terry was thrilled when Mother told him that she and Dad would consider extending their stay, and he invited them to be his guests in his home while he was away. He arranged for his Japanese gardener to continue his services, handed my folks the keys to the house, and departed on his tour. Mother invited our family to come visit and see Honolulu and some of the rest of Oahu. Sid was unable to go because the Bexar County Medical Association was in the process of building a new headquarters, and he had to be available to handle any problems with its construction. However, Carol, Cathy, and I were delighted to accept.

We traveled to Los Angeles by train, watching the scenery of the great Southwest pass by our window. We had a compartment in a Pullman car, where the seats converted into beds, carefully made up at night by the train's conductor, and we dined in a car with white linen tablecloths and gourmet food. Train travel then was different from riding the rails on Amtrak as we know it today. In Los Angeles we transferred to the airport and arrived in Honolulu late in the evening. Mother and Dad met us with fragrant plumeria leis and drove us to the beautiful estate where they were living. The next morning, after breakfast, we walked through a garden of mango, papaya, and guava trees, sprays of blooming orchids, birds-of-paradise, and other tropical flowers. We had a gorgeous view of the waterfront from our hilltop. Later we explored Honolulu, saw the International Marketplace, and ventured to the other side of Oahu in Dad's car. We all agreed that Mother had come up with a great idea when she insisted they visit Hawaii after Dad's retirement. Later Carol told me that the trip had opened her eyes to a bigger world made up of diverse ethnicities and cultures.

～

In the early 1960s San Antonio was recognizing its unique blend of ethnicities and cultures as well. With nearly 44 percent of the population of Latino descent, quinceañeras, charro rodeos, and all kinds of fiestas were joyful events with Hispanic origins, enjoyed by all.

We had a party of our own in March 1961, when Mom and Dad Cockrell celebrated their fiftieth wedding anniversary. With the help of Sid's brother, Tracy, and his wife, Kay, who lived in Midland, we planned a huge gathering at our home on Mary Louise Drive. Not unlike a quinceañera, it included family members and friends from all over Texas and Oklahoma. Mom Cockrell was beaming all afternoon, and Dad Cockrell was overcome with emotion when he saw how many relatives had come for the celebration.

～

In my second two-year term as president of the League of Women Voters, I wanted to be sure Carol and Cathy were being introduced to the responsibilities of being a good citizen and keeping up with civic and governmental affairs, so I arranged to take them to Austin when the state legislature was in session. I had called ahead to state senator Franklin Spears's office to arrange for passes to the senate gallery, and he was a gracious host. He personally took us on a tour of the capitol building and seated us in the gallery in time to witness Sen. "Red" Berry of San Antonio read his mail. The local newspapers had recently run a coupon accompanied by a message from the Milk Producers of America asking citizens to sign the coupon and mail it to their state senators urging their support of a particular piece of legislation. Evidently Senator Berry was not pleased with the huge mountain of mail that had resulted; he was seated with his feet on his desk and a large wastebasket at his side. He went through an elaborate exercise of holding each piece of mail up to the light, and if he saw a coupon inside the envelope, he leaned over and threw it unopened into the wastebasket. That was not the civic lesson I had in mind for my daughters that day.

My own civic duties now included participation on the Council of International Relations, headed by Mrs. Preston Dial, "Miss Mamie" to her friends. She was a San Antonio treasure, and her organization extended hospitality to foreign visitors, including military officers from other countries who were attending English language classes at Lackland Air Force Base. Miss Mamie would host large lawn parties at her beautiful home in Olmos Park, with food, fellowship, and lots of fun. The fun part usually started with a "branding ceremony" whereby officers from other countries would be branded honorary Texans. She referred to the young officers she branded as "my boys," and they seemed to love the warmth of her hospitality. I served as the secretary of her council, and years later, after I became the mayor of San Antonio, she always referred to me as "my secretary."

The annual Black and White Ball was founded by Mrs. Maria Magnon to promote friendship between Mexico and the United States, with a high-ranking Mexican official and a high-ranking U.S. official as the honored guests. Young ladies were presented at the ball, representing Mexican civic and social organizations and San Antonio organizations. In fall 1961 Miss Mamie invited Carol to represent the Council of International Relations as a princess at the ball. Participation meant an exciting round of social events, and each organization sponsoring a princess held a tea, reception, or other party in her honor. The ball took place in December in Municipal Auditorium, and Carol's great-grandmother, Julia

My grandmother, Julia McCampbell, came to San Antonio in 1961 for the Black and White Ball, where Carol (*far right*) was a princess; Cathy (*far left*) was presented several years later.

McCampbell, came from Fort Worth for the gala evening. Carol looked beautiful and executed her onstage bow perfectly; all of us were proud of her. Cathy took note of everything, hoping for a similar invitation in the future.

I was thinking about the future too. I'd been

watching a rather new civic organization with growing interest, aware that it was gaining political clout in San Antonio. The Good Government League, or GGL, was established after community leaders who had led the successful movement to get a new city charter approved in 1951 recognized that San Antonio's change to a council-manager form of government was not experiencing an easy transition. The first two elected city councils had struggled with controversy and recall petitions. Business leaders formed the GGL to stabilize the new city government process, setting up procedures to select and recruit candidates for city council, field a ticket, raise the necessary funds for the campaign, and work to elect the candidates they had chosen.

The first GGL-backed council took office in 1955 and was headed by Mayor Ed Kuykendall. Members of the media nicknamed him Chuckhole Eddy because San Antonio had so many problems with street repairs. The mayor and his wife, Oleta, lived in our neighborhood and attended the same church we did. Oleta Kuykendall was a tall, striking lady who was famous in the city for her large collection of beautiful, wide-brimmed hats that she wore to all occasions. After they moved to a spacious house in Monte Vista, I attended a ladies' tea party there, and all the ladies were invited upstairs to view Oleta's closet. In those days most closets were small; Oleta's was nearly the size of a room. There were shelves for her hats, purses, and accessories, and all her dresses were hung on racks. We were impressed and just a wee bit envious!

~

In 1961 Walter W. McAllister, a prominent business leader who headed the San Antonio Savings Association, became the leader of the GGL ticket and was elected mayor. During that election year, a conservationist named Wanda Ford ran a strong campaign as an independent candidate and came close to winning a seat on the city council, which was comprised of nine men. She scared those men, and I realized later that her race most certainly got the GGL leadership's attention and led to their decision to put a woman on the ticket in 1963. McAllister proved to be a very strong mayor, with powerful support from the business community and the general public. Although service on the city council was nonpartisan, Mayor Mac was known to be a staunch Republican.

About this time San Antonio was beginning to look at the possibility of holding a world's fair. Local businessman Jerome Harris had suggested the idea as a celebration of San Antonio's 250th birthday; it was also hoped that it would be a way to restore some of the retail business and tourism that had left San Antonio for cities like Houston and Dallas. The idea languished until U.S. Congressman Henry B. González became interested and asked his friend, businessman Bill Sinkin, to pursue it. It would take several years before the idea gained momentum, eventually transforming San Antonio into an international city.

Another issue was smoldering in San Antonio, and in many other cities in America—segregation. The civil rights movement brought much-needed attention to the issue, and as host to five military bases that made major contributions to the local economy, San Antonio leaders realized there was strong federal interest in resolving it.

In January 1963 I received an intriguing phone call from Mayor McAllister. He asked if he and a small group of men could call on me. I agreed, of course, and was curious about what would be discussed. On the afternoon of the meeting, I peeped out of the living room window and saw two cars pulling up to the house. Four or five men got out of each car, and Mayor McAllister led the group into my living room. They stated their mission; they were inviting

The civil rights movement brought much-needed attention to the national problem of segregation in the early 1960s.

me to be the first woman on the GGL ticket in the 1963 election for city council.

I told them I was very flattered and appreciative but that I had a few questions. First I wanted to know a bit more about how campaigns were run and what my personal obligations would be. And I wanted to know, assuming a successful election, if anyone would tell me how I was expected to vote on future issues.

The answer to the first question was that the GGL candidates would run as a team, with the mayor as the leader. The GGL would handle scheduling, overall campaign themes, and all of the fundraising. The answer to the second question was that no one would tell me how I was expected to vote. I was told that the GGL worked hard to select qualified candidates and expected them to use their best judgment on the issues. The answers were reassuring, and I was very interested, but I needed to talk it over with my husband and family before accepting. I told the mayor I would be in touch with him in the next few days.

That evening I discussed the invitation with Sid and the girls. Sid immediately understood that this was something I would really like to do and that a resignation from the League of Women Voters would be necessary because of that organization's nonpartisan rules. He may also have thought it would not involve any more time than I was spending in my role as president of that group. The girls were a little uncertain; nobody else's mother had ever run for public office, and they worried I might be involved in controversy. I was touched by their concern, but with Sid's blessing I called the mayor and accepted the invitation.

I resigned from the League of Women Voters. Since my term as president was coming to an end, my successor, Dorie Clark, had already been selected; the transition was an easy one. I began reviewing the pending issues before the city council, realizing the media might ask for my opinion once my candidacy was announced. As it turned out, there was quite a bit of media interest in the fact that there would be a "new face" on the GGL ticket, and that it would be a woman. One of my first interviews, which was televised, was with Paul Thompson, a columnist for the *San Antonio Express-News*. For his final question, he asked, "Mrs. Cockrell, the GGL is thought to be weak in its support on the East Side and West Side. What are you going to do about that?"

"Well, Paul," I said, "if that is where we are weak, that is where we will have to try harder."

I enjoyed campaigning. I realized it was a big advantage to run on the GGL ticket, with committees in place to help organize and fund the campaign. At that time there were nine members of the city council, including the mayor, and we all ran at large. When our GGL group went to city hall to register as candidates, I was photographed amid eight men, wearing a navy-blue suit, navy-blue straw hat, and white gloves. Something new was happening in city politics. But in that election, and in the next two, I registered as Mrs. S. E. Cockrell Jr. It was not until the 1969 campaign that I registered as Lila Cockrell.

～

The citywide campaign we conducted in 1963 was an educational experience, and my high school and college debate experience and various civic leadership roles gave me confidence. I enjoyed going to neighborhoods, meeting people in all parts of the city, and trying to get my campaign message across. I not only had the opportunity to speak; I also was able to listen, and I heard from voters in these different neighborhoods about their priorities and concerns. I spoke to many women's organizations that wanted to hear from the first woman candidate, and many friends held coffees and receptions for me in their neighborhoods. I had only token opposition—one candidate who filed fifteen minutes before the deadline. In a media interview he commented, "Mrs. Cockrell would have to murder her husband or commit some other occurrence for me to have a chance at being elected, but I felt that she should have some opposition." Of course, no dire event took place, and our entire ticket was elected.

I was touched by the congratulatory cards and letters I received from friends and acquaintances in the community and from other elected officials. I knew that I would have to dedicate myself to working hard and trying my best to serve in the public interest, and I was ready to meet that challenge. I knew too that as the first woman to serve under the GGL leadership (although two women had brief tenures in an earlier time), I had to excel so others could follow this path of opportunity. The San Antonio River would remain my inspiration and guide star—a symbolic ribbon of water that united some very diverse neighborhoods and city council districts. City council members were paid $20 after each meeting, and the mayor received an extra $50, not to exceed $1,080 a year. We were not in this for the money.

SEVEN

Eight Gentlemen and a Madam

1963–68

A spray of beautiful flowers was at my place at the city council table on May 1, 1963—something new in those hallowed halls. After roll call by City Clerk Jake Inselmann, who announced that a quorum was present, my first council meeting began. In the past, the meetings had opened with the salutation "Gentlemen." For the first time in San Antonio's history, that was amended to "Gentlemen and Madam." I was proud and thrilled to be there, and I resolved to be a truly effective councilwoman, an example to other women who would want to serve on the council in the future.

I realized that I had a lot to learn. I was a homemaker and civic leader who had dealt with issues and causes, but the business side of cities was something new. I needed to learn quickly since discussions of the city budget would take place shortly after I took

I was elected to the city council as Mrs. S. E. Cockrell Jr.;
I would serve several terms before running as Lila Cockrell.

office. I've always believed that it is best to be honest
and admit when I am not familiar with something,
and that I need help to get up to speed, rather than
trying to bluff my way through. I asked lots of
questions and carefully studied the processes used

I was the only woman on the city council in 1963; other members were (*left to right*) Jack Kaufman, Bob Jones, George De La Garza, Mayor McAllister, Ronald Bremer, Gerald Parker, Roy Padilla, and John Gatti.

to handle city business, as well as the council's role relative to the city manager and other staff.

While the proposed city budget is prepared by the city manager and staff, the city council must give policy direction on its priorities. For me, the budget process quickly became the most challenging part of my responsibilities. In college I had taken a liberal arts curriculum and had not taken any business school courses. At home my husband, Sid, who had a degree in business administration, took the leadership role on family finances. When I was confronted with my first thick copy of what, in retrospect, was a very modest city budget, I immediately set up extra sessions with staff members from the finance office. I studied that document so carefully, and I looked at other city budgets around the state. Soon I felt comfortable holding my own budget discussions.

I also worked hard to become better acquainted with the other council members. Although I had started that process while on the campaign trail, I wanted to probe deeper to learn about each council member's ideas, positions, and concerns regarding the items on our agenda. They came from diverse backgrounds and professions. Mayor McAllister was chairman of the San Antonio Savings Association board and was well known in financial and business circles. John Gatti, who served as mayor pro tem, headed an investment firm. Dr. Gerald Parker was a veterinarian with a practice on the city's South Side, and Jack Kaufman was an attorney. George De La Garza was an automobile salesman, and Roy Padilla was a small business owner. Roland Bremer was the bishop of the Mormon Church in San Antonio, while Claus Rohlfs was a Methodist minister. Each brought special talents to the council, and as I got to know my fellow council members, I came to appreciate their diverse skills and opinions.

I especially got a kick out of George De La Garza, who was a great storyteller. He was rather short in stature and a little on the pudgy side, but he always described himself as "that tall dark Latin lover." One of the great stories he told was about the time he accompanied the men on the city council to the Texas coast, at the invitation of Mayor Mac, who had a summer home in Port Aransas. The mayor had chartered a fishing boat to take the party out into the Gulf of Mexico for some deep-sea fishing. No sooner were they out in deep water than George became seasick. He stretched out on the deck feeling miserable, and one of the other men brought him a fishing rod, all rigged up, and put it in his hand. George accepted it without enthusiasm, but soon there was a distinct tug on the line. Still feeling ill, he managed to sit up and with some help pulled in a very nice catch. A crew member took charge of the fish, and George stretched out again. Soon the fishing rod was put in his hand again, and before long there was another tug on his line. At this point no one else had caught anything, so some of the others rushed over to cheer on George. He forced himself to sit up once more and bring in the fish, another nice catch. George's two fish were the only ones caught that day.

When they returned to shore, George was directed to a fish-processing business where his bounty would be cleaned and frozen. The group returned to Mayor Mac's Port Aransas house and enjoyed a nice dinner before heading back to San Antonio. George did not give his fish another thought. Later that evening, after he had arrived at home and was settled in bed, the doorbell rang. It was a delivery person from an air express company, bringing the fish accompanied by a COD charge of $50. George paid the bill, put the fish in the refrigerator, and went back to bed. Then, as George told the story, two days later his wife, Olivia, said to him, "What are you going to do with those fish?" A distinct odor permeated the refrigerator and kitchen. The fish were thrown out, and Mayor Mac, who loved to go deep-sea fishing, was never able to convert George into an enthusiastic fisherman.

While I never went fishing with Mayor Mac, I did accompany him to many ceremonial appearances and ribbon cuttings to open stores and parks and schools. Since the men on the council had full-time professional obligations and my time was more flexible, I was often the one who attended these events.

I enjoyed them. They gave me the opportunity to meet more citizens and become acquainted with more businesses in the city.

Soon after joining the council, I became interested in a major issue being discussed at the city water board, a plan for developing a new surface water supply for San Antonio. The idea to develop a dam at Canyon Lake had been proposed in the late 1950s, and San Antonio had been in competition with the Guadalupe-Blanco River Authority (GBRA) for the rights to build that dam. But the GBRA was awarded the rights, and San Antonio leaders were still smarting from the loss.

A proposal was developed by the San Antonio River Authority (SARA) in partnership with the GBRA to build two dams on the Guadalupe River near Cuero, Texas. A third dam would be built at Cibolo with a connecting pipeline system that would bring water to San Antonio, where a treatment plant would be built to process the water before it was added to the municipal water supply. The proposal suggested three phases, starting with Cuero I, the first dam in Cuero. It would have been a large and expensive project, but ultimately it would have provided a significant supply of additional water to San Antonio.

I became interested in the proposal, realizing that we needed to be more proactive in projecting and preparing for San Antonio's future growth, and specifically the need for additional sources to supplement the water we take from the Edwards Aquifer. But I also realized that Mayor Mac was not a fan of the proposal. I think he felt that we should take the less expensive water from the Edwards Aquifer for as long as possible, to keep control of as much of that water as we could for San Antonio's present and future use. It also seemed to me that he was still hoping that someday San Antonio would be able to get water from Canyon Lake, and he did not like the idea of having the Guadalupe River flow down to Cuero, to be impounded in a reservoir that would be created by the proposed Cuero I dam, and then having to pay the costs of pumping that water to Cibolo before pumping it back to San Antonio. The mayor may also have known that the city water board hoped to gain approval to build its own dams on three rivers north of San Antonio—the Guadalupe, Blanco, and Pedernales—as an alternative approach.

I felt the SARA-GBRA proposal was worthy of further study, but I was a neophyte member of the council, still on a learning curve in city government. I did not feel ready to step forward to champion this cause, and in July the city council turned down the proposal, and San Antonio withdrew from the project. The city water board began to work for council approval to proceed with plans for constructing the three dams to the north, but the plan could not gain approval, and the dams were never built.

During my first year on the council, I experienced some important changes on the home front, reminders that life is a series of losses and beginnings. My beloved grandmother, Julia "Muddie" McCampbell, passed away in Fort Worth, where she had still managed her apartment house at age eighty-four, despite a recent illness. I had the chance to visit her often during the last few months of her life, to remember the many adventures we shared, and to thank her for important life lessons she had instilled in me. Meanwhile Carol was graduating from Jefferson High School and preparing to enter Southwestern University in Georgetown; a new phase of her life was beginning. That summer we assembled her college wardrobe, purchased items for her dorm room, and talked about the upcoming sorority rush week, just as I had done with my grandmother before I went to SMU so many years before. Life does come full circle.

There was a departure on the city council as well.

Claus Rohlfs was being transferred to another church and would soon be leaving San Antonio; he resigned his council position in September. We were approaching a vote on a controversial issue on which the council was divided, five to four, and I worried that his important vote would be lost. We had been discussing a proposal to authorize the San Antonio Housing Authority to develop additional public housing units, and I felt strongly that this was needed. San Antonio had a large number of families with incomes below the poverty level who were having trouble finding affordable private sector housing. Five of us were in favor of the proposal, including Claus. The San Antonio Home Builders and real estate boards strongly opposed the measure, and Mayor Mac agreed with the opposition. Usually when the mayor had a strong opinion on an issue, council members were inclined to agree with him.

We needed Claus's vote. On the afternoon of his last meeting, we insisted the vote be taken. Mayor Mac wished to postpone the vote until a new council member was on board, but the five of us stood firm, and the authorization was approved. Robert C. "Bob" Jones, a realtor, was appointed to replace Claus, and he respected the decision and never tried to get it rescinded.

President and Mrs. John F. Kennedy and Texas Governor and Mrs. John Connally visited San Antonio just one day before the president was assassinated in Dallas in 1963.

In November San Antonio was looking forward to the visit of President and Mrs. John F. Kennedy. City council members were invited to attend and sit in special reserved seats when Kennedy spoke at Brooks Air Force Base on November 21. We received detailed instructions, and I arrived well ahead of time and took my seat. George De La Garza, on the other hand, barely arrived in time. He explained that he had mistakenly wandered into the area where President Kennedy and the other dignitaries were waiting to go onstage, and he was euphoric about his up close and personal encounter.

The next day I was at home doing housework when the telephone rang shortly after noon. It was George. In a shocked voice, he asked me if I had my television turned on. He told me that President Kennedy had been shot while riding in his open car in a Dallas motorcade. I ran into the den, turned on our television set, and along with millions of other Americans watched with horror and sadness as the tragic news unfolded. After the official announcement that the president had died, I continued to watch as Vice President Lyndon B. Johnson was administered the oath of office as president of the United States on Air Force One by my Dallas friend Judge Sarah T. Hughes.

Later I learned that my mother and father had driven to Dallas from Fort Worth to view the motorcade. They stood outside the Dallas Athletic Club, where they had guest privileges through their membership at the Fort Worth Club, waving to the president as he went by. They went inside the building and rode the elevator to the club floor to have lunch. When they exited the elevator, they saw people gathered around a television and learned that the president had been shot and was on his way to the hospital. The country went into mourning. Most people who witnessed the television coverage of the assassination, the funeral, and the transition of power to a new president recall it as one of the saddest moments in our nation's history.

Even after tragedies like this, life goes on. Cathy got her turn to participate in the Black and White Ball in December. It appeared that this would be the last time the ball was held, and it was renamed the Maria Magnon Memorial Ball in honor of its founder. Like Carol two years before, Cathy spent long hours practicing her deep presentation bow. As princess of San Antonio she was feted at a reception at the Saint Anthony Hotel. Gertrude Passur, the wife of former city councilman Mike Passur, hosted the party, and Mrs. Walter McAllister, wife of Mayor Mac, presided at the tea table.

With a daughter in college, we were on a tight budget, so I altered and enhanced the same ball gown that Carol had worn two years before—adding more glitter and sequins—for Cathy's big night. The ball was held in December at Municipal Auditorium, and Mayor and Mrs. McAllister were guests at our table. At the end of the evening, the judges' selection of the queen of the Black and White Ball was announced. It was our Cathy!

Cathy was involved in the usual activities of a teenager in the 1960s. She served on the junior board at Rhodes Department Store, where she worked on Saturdays during the school year and more hours during the summer. She used her earnings and her store discount to buy her complete wardrobe for her freshman year at Texas Christian University (TCU). She was also a finalist in the Miss Teena Texas competition sponsored by Joske's Department Store. Located on the corner of Alamo and Commerce Streets, Joske's had a long history in San Antonio, dating back to 1867. In the 1930s it became the first fully air-conditioned store in Texas and the first to install escalators; until 1987 it was the largest department store west of the Mississippi River. During the Christmas holidays, Joske's converted its fourth floor into "Fantasyland," and a forty-foot-tall Santa waved from the store's rooftop. Visiting Fantasyland and the spectacular holiday windows was an annual highlight for families during the 1950s and 1960s.

Beneath the twinkle of Joske's lights, there was a dark side to the story. Until summer 1960, only whites could eat in the three restaurants inside the store. That seems incredible to us now, but segregation was a terrible reality less than sixty years ago. Sadly, Joske's was just one example.

Despite the twinkling Christmas lights and forty-foot-tall
Santa at Joske's, the state's largest department store, the issue
of race relations had finally emerged from the shadows, and
San Antonio citizens realized that changes were long overdue.

By the early 1960s issues regarding race relations
were coming up more frequently at council meetings. G.J. Sutton, a leader in the African American
community, was a frequent visitor in our chambers.
His parents were both educators, and he was one of
fifteen children, all of whom graduated from high
school. One brother owned the famous Apollo Theater in New York City and was the attorney for Mal-
colm X, and another was a judge on the New York

G. J. Sutton, a business leader on the East Side, was an important voice promoting representation in city government from all sectors of the city.

Supreme Court. G. J. Sutton and another brother owned and operated a mortuary on San Antonio's East Side. When he visited the city council, he was often accompanied by a young up-and-coming community leader, the Rev. Claude Black, who was pastor of Mount Zion First Baptist Church. On one visit they were accompanied by a local labor official, and they lodged a complaint about the lack of African Americans in city government leadership positions.

I was sympathetic to their concerns. I asked the labor
union representative how many African Americans
were members of the union. He had to report that
there were none.

Thankfully things were changing, but it would be
nearly a decade before Sutton was elected as a state
representative, in 1972, becoming the first African
American from San Antonio to hold that office. The
city council, however, moved more quickly. When
the GGL began preparing for city elections in 1965,
George De La Garza submitted his resignation and
was replaced by Dr. Herbert Calderón, a dentist.
Two other candidates were on the ticket—Felix B.
Treviño, a West Side businessman who replaced Roy
Padilla, and the Rev. S. H. James, pastor of the Second Baptist Church on the East Side, who replaced
Jack Kaufman. The GGL had decided it was time to
run someone from San Antonio's African American
community, and Reverend James was their choice.
The Second Baptist Church was home to one of the
largest African American congregations in the city;
its beautiful building had been designed by the prestigious architectural firm Ford, Powell & Carson.
The lead architect on the project was Norcell Haywood, who was a church member. The GGL's slate
was elected, and members of the new council were

Mayor McAllister, John Gatti, Bob Jones, Dr. Gerald Parker, Dr. Herbert Calderón, Roland Bremer, Felix Treviño, the Rev. S. H. James, and me.

~

During my early years on the council, I had my first taste of international diplomacy. I received a telephone call from Mayor McAllister informing me that the governor of the Mexican state of Jalisco and his wife were coming to San Antonio for an official visit, in connection with our Sister City relationship with Guadalajara. Mayor Mac's wife was out of town, and he asked if I would serve as hostess to the governor's wife during the visit.

We arrived at the Saint Anthony Hotel, where the delegation was staying, promptly at 10 a.m. and found the governor and several other men waiting for us. Knowing that the mayor had arranged for one car to take us on a tour of the city, I whispered to him, asking if he thought the extra gentlemen were expecting to accompany us on the tour. Mayor Mac discreetly asked the governor, and it turned out they were all expecting to see the city. The mayor excused himself for a moment and went inside to request a second car and police escort. About that time the governor's wife arrived along with three other ladies.

Sizing up the situation, Mayor Mac excused himself again and made a call for a third car and escort. While we were waiting for the cars to arrive, we posed with our guests for official photographs.

As soon as the cars arrived, Mayor Mac started leading the delegation to the front door of the hotel, eager to get the show on the road. One of the ladies who spoke English caught my arm and said that there was a problem. None of the ladies had eaten breakfast yet. I explained the situation to the mayor and offered to take the ladies to the Saint Anthony Hotel's coffee shop and then to catch up with the tour as quickly as possible. Mayor Mac and the gentlemen departed in two cars, leaving one car and police escort behind, along with a two-way radio to communicate with the entourage. The ladies enjoyed a leisurely breakfast. Just as I was about to suggest we catch up with the men, one of the ladies informed me that whenever the governor's wife went on an official tour, it was customary for her to visit an orphanage, senior citizens' home, or similar facility. I excused myself and made a quick call to the manager's office at the San Antonio Housing Authority's newest senior citizens' home, the Marie Maguire Apartments, a high-rise building in the nearby Victoria Courts neighborhood. I asked if they could arrange a tour and a Spanish language interpreter with just a few minutes' notice. Miraculously they rose to the occasion and we had a lovely tour, where the governor's wife was photographed meeting many of the senior citizen residents.

As we made our way back to the car, everyone was happy. Before I could ask our police officer and driver to let the mayor know we would soon be joining the group, the ladies looked at me with big smiles and said, "Now we'll go shopping." I made another hasty revision to the plan. We headed for Joske's and spent the rest of the day there. We never caught up with the mayor's group, but I knew my assignment had been successfully completed. With all the shopping that took place at Joske's, I was certain the store executives were delighted with the improvised schedule.

~

This experience was the first of many times when I interacted with official groups from Mexico, often from our Sister Cities of Guadalajara and Monterrey. In turn I was privileged to be part of reciprocal visits to those cities, as well as to Mexico City. Since so many of our San Antonio citizens were descendants of families that originated in Mexico, I felt it was important to learn about the country to our south and its rich history and culture. Sid shared my interest because in addition to duties at the Bexar County Medical Society, he served as executive secretary of the International Medical Society of Southwest Texas. In that role he planned tours and social events, arranged exchange visits with physicians in Mexico, and attended annual seminars with Mexican doctors in cities and resort areas in Mexico. We had both come to appreciate the multicultural aspects of San Antonio, and we loved exploring their origins.

Beautiful plazas, parks, and gardens are very much a part of city landscapes in Mexico, and San Antonio has incorporated them into its urban planning as well. Miraflores, the historic garden constructed by Dr. Aureliano Urrutia in 1921, is a wonderful example. Dr. Urrutia came to San Antonio from Mexico in 1914, and seven years later he started what would be a twenty-year project on 4.5 acres just below the headwaters of the San Antonio River. Its spectacular concrete and mosaic arch, sculptures, walkways, and other objects in the garden reflect aspects of Mexican art and culture. And, of course, I knew the stories about the Japanese Tea Garden, reflecting a different history and culture, remembering that my parents strolled there as young newlyweds. As the only woman on the council, it seemed natural that I would gravitate toward an interest in parks and city beautification.

I became interested in the efforts of the Beautify San Antonio Association, founded by O. P. Schnabel, a prominent hardware store owner who referred to himself as Old Pushbroom. He and his wife had toured Europe, and they were tremendously impressed with the cleanliness and beauty of the cities in Switzerland. When they returned to San Antonio, O.P. had found his civic cause. He had business cards printed with his name and the slogan "Be a beauty bug, not a litterbug." He attached a penny to each card to be sure its recipient noticed it, and he was famous for stopping his car to pick up annoying bits of litter on the roadways.

My interest in the beautification of San Antonio led Mayor Mac to designate me as the city's representative at the National Cleanest Town conference in Washington, DC, where San Antonio would be recognized at the closing dinner. My flight schedule involved a change of planes in Houston. I was concerned because we had a tight connection and our plane was late leaving San Antonio. We barely made our Houston plane for Washington, but my luggage did not make it. The Eastern Airlines baggage room attendant was very upbeat, assuring me that my lug-

gage would be on the next flight and would be delivered to my hotel room at the Capitol Hilton. I took a
cab to the hotel and checked in. After freshening up
in my room, without any luggage to unpack, I went
down to the lobby to meet the other San Antonio
delegates attending the conference.

A little while later I returned to my room to see
if my bag had been delivered. When I inserted my
key in the lock of my room door, I couldn't open
it. Suddenly a woman in a bathrobe opened the
door, asking what I wanted. I could hear the shower
running. I explained this was the room I had been
assigned when I checked in two hours ago. She said
she and her roommate had been assigned the room
an hour ago and invited me to come inside to call the
front desk. When I called, the desk clerk was very
apologetic and said he would give me the first available room; every room was occupied at the moment!

The ladies who had now showered and unpacked
in the room were attending a conference for home
economics teachers. They graciously allowed me to
stay until the hotel found me another room. Next
I called Eastern Airlines to see if my luggage had
arrived. It had not. I finally got a new hotel room
about 5 p.m.; another check with Eastern Airlines
revealed that my bag had been found—in Atlanta,

Georgia! Fortunately I had on a tailored navy-blue suit instead of something more casual, because that was what I wore to the awards dinner as well. The next day I finally received my luggage, thirty minutes before leaving the hotel to come home. A lesson was learned: take carry-on luggage when you are traveling for a short time!

Back in San Antonio, the beautification movement continued. The city entered into a contract with the Dallas-based firm John Watson Landscape Illumination for a pilot project to illuminate the trees in one block of the Paseo del Rio, or River Walk. In a B Session meeting, when informal, in-depth discussion takes place in preparation for a council meeting, I suggested that since the First Lady had been so active in beautification projects, we should invite her to San Antonio to throw the switch on the lighting that would enhance a portion of our river. The idea was not met with much enthusiasm, perhaps because it seemed unlikely that Lady Bird Johnson would come. But no one objected to my sending an invitation, and I immediately wrote to Mrs. Johnson expressing appreciation for all that she had done to beautify our country.

Several weeks later I received a telephone call from Liz Carpenter, press secretary and staff director for

Lady Bird Johnson, the First Lady (*center*), visited San Antonio in 1966 to celebrate our Cleanest City award.

Mrs. Johnson. She told me that the First Lady was considering accepting my invitation, and I was invited to the White House to discuss details and planning. I was tremendously excited when a follow-up letter arrived with specific instructions to come to the east gate of the White House on Monday, February 14, at 9:30 a.m. A guard would show me to Liz's office on the second floor. During that special visit to the First Lady's office suite, her staff and I developed the framework for her visit to San Antonio, and I went home with some follow-up work to complete.

After several rounds of telephone calls and correspondence, the schedule was approved, arrangements were made, and the event took place on the evening of April 1, 1966. I had invited Gov. John and Nellie Connally to join us for the event. The governor could not attend, but his wife, our Texas first lady, came from Austin, along with the speaker of the Texas House of Representatives, Ben Barnes, and his wife, Martha. The lighting ceremony took place close to the Arneson River Theatre. After the First Lady greeted and spoke to the crowd, she turned on the switch, illuminating the river in a spectacular wash of lights.

We boarded three barges to continue the adventure. On the first barge Lady Bird Johnson, Nellie Connally, Mayor McAllister, and I, along with several others, led the way, enchanted by the new lights. The second barge held the press corps from Washington and Texas and other accredited media, and the third barge was occupied by the rest of the city council, other invited guests, and John Watson, the lighting designer. As we cruised down the river, with several stops along the way, musical groups positioned on bridges or the adjacent sidewalk serenaded the First

Lady. The evening concluded with a beautiful dinner and reception. I remember the experience as truly magical and still feel that magic whenever I am near the San Antonio River.

Building on Lady Bird Johnson's visit, with city council approval, I organized Beautify San Antonio: Invitation to Action at the convention center. The conference offered a variety of workshops and opportunities for further improvements and actions; more than three hundred people participated. The city, the Urban Renewal Agency, the San Antonio River Authority, and other public sector groups worked alongside private sector business and civic organizations, including the San Antonio Chamber of Commerce and Beautify San Antonio. The conference received national recognition, and the official publication of the National League of Cities featured a photograph of the San Antonio River near the restaurant Casa Rio, with the headline "Beauty in the City—San Antonio Still Sets the Pace." The article reported on Lady Bird Johnson's visit and the follow-up conference. I was especially gratified by the last two lines: "Beautification needs a woman's touch. This extra ingredient has been supplied by San Antonio's Councilwoman, Mrs. S. E. Cockrell Jr."

Later that fall, with the river still very much on

my mind, I helped launch the first barge in the city's new fleet of river "party barges" by cracking a bottle of champagne over the side, wearing what was then a stylish straw hat and white gloves. The Paseo del Rio Association held a contest to name that first barge in the new fleet, and on September 19 the local newspapers announced that the barge would be named the *Ms. Lila.*

Patricia Anderson, who submitted the winning name in the contest, accompanied Sid and me on a dinner cruise along the lighted Paseo del Rio waterway. I was so touched and honored to have that first barge named for me. My happiness was doubled when I saw the excitement and pride on the faces of my daughters when they took their first ride on the *Ms. Lila.*

Both girls were now in college, and both were members of the sorority I had joined several decades ago. Sid and I followed their adventures and accomplishments with pride, and I was careful to balance my role as a mother with my role as a city councilwoman.

Balance was not always possible on the city council. I was the lone no vote on a rate hike requested by the city water board in 1966; I thought other alternatives had not been explored carefully enough. And I was one of only two council members who attended a special meeting hosted by Congressman Henry B. González to discuss San Antonio's participation in a new federal program called Model Cities.

The program began in 1966, when Lyndon Johnson was president. Five U.S. cities would be designated Model Cities after a careful selection process. Congressman González, who was a close friend of the president, came to town to tell the council about the opportunities the program might offer San Antonio. Mayor McAllister did not like the program and did not want San Antonio to participate. He did not go to the meeting, nor did most of the other council members. Councilman Bob Jones attended with me, but not because he was going to support the project. My position was that since Congress had already put the program in place and the money was going to be spent, San Antonio should try to get its share. We were not a wealthy city, and if the federal government was going to put millions of dollars into the redevelopment of cities, we needed to be one of the Model Cities. I did not let my own conservative opinions about national politics or partisanship stand in the way of going after money San Antonio needed—I was "in" for San Antonio.

I kept pushing and pressuring my fellow council

members. Finally we did send in our application, but it was late in the game. When the first five cities were announced, we weren't included, because we had not applied in time. But because of Congressman González and President Johnson, San Antonio was added as a sixth Model City.

The millions of federal dollars awarded to the Model Cities would be used for road improvements, housing, flood control, economic development projects, school projects, and more. The program required each city to establish an organization called the Citizens Policy Participation Committee (CPPC) with representatives elected from the communities within the Model Cities designated area. This group would serve as a review board for the proposed projects, so decisions were not left entirely to city hall. This was San Antonio's nascent citizen participation effort. For the first time, citizens were energized and mobilized to help develop public policy.

The CPPC subcommittees had to work with each other to reach their goals. The housing subcommittee was pushing for more multifamily housing in underdeveloped areas, but the education subcommittee was working with school districts that were questioning the addition of the housing, because they did not know how they would accommodate, and pay for, the resulting increase in students. Citizens had to grapple with sometimes competing goals and find a resolution to complex problems, with a better understanding of how issues are interconnected.

The Model Cities program brought a lot of resources to San Antonio's West Side, including important funding to ameliorate the flooding at the Alazán-Apache Creek housing project and money for school districts and neighborhood businesses. I remain grateful to Henry B. González for his push for San Antonio to be in the program; he cared deeply about his constituents, had great integrity, and was warm and welcoming. We became good friends. He always volunteered to take me to the airport when I was in Washington on official business. I was never thrilled with his offer, because it meant a hurried, last-minute ride, and I was afraid I would miss my plane, but I never did. He always got me there, just barely in time. The airlines were used to holding the doors for him—which was still possible in those days prior to modern security rules—but it was always a tense ride!

~

San Antonio was booming, and I cut the ribbon for many building projects, including a $220,000 addition at the San Antonio Transit System, a San Antonio Garden Center building in Mahncke Park, a ground breaking for the Protestant Children's Home, the opening of the San Antonio Conservation Society's Old San Antonio museum at Bolivar Hall in La Villita, and the grand opening of the 1.62-million-cubic-foot W&W bonded warehouse on the Pan Am Expressway. Of course, my favorite was being the official designated to throw the switch to light the city's huge Christmas tree in Alamo Plaza, ushering in the holidays. At home we installed our own tall tree in our two-story living room. Carol and Cathy were home for the holidays, and family and friends gathered to sing and celebrate.

~

Another celebration had been in the planning stages for several years. San Antonio would mark its 250th birthday in 1968, and an ambitious plan to host a "world's fair of the Americas" had been developing. We all were aware of the great impact that HemisFair would have on our city, with millions of visitors— and dollars—expected, new buildings and amenities to showcase San Antonio and generate tourism, and visibility as an international city. City officials and private citizens partnered in the dream, working on securing accreditation as a sanctioned fair, seeking federal and state approval and participation, soliciting other countries and major corporations to sponsor pavilions and exhibits, getting a site plan designed, undertaking urban renewal, awarding construction contracts, and of course, major fundraising. The theme of the international exposition would be A Confluence of Cultures in the Americas, and San Antonio, with its multicultural heritage, was the perfect place to showcase this important message.

I was appointed to serve as chair of the coordinating committee, which included representatives from the city council, the HemisFair executive committee, and the Urban Renewal Agency. The coordinating committee's job was to work on issues that needed the cooperation of all three groups and to keep communications flowing freely to avoid the problems that result when groups do not talk to one another.

The City of San Antonio was responsible for financing and building what would be the "theme structure" for the fair, the Tower of the Americas. The plan was for the city to issue revenue bonds that would be repaid from admission charges for access to the observation and dining levels of the tower. Mayor Mac gave me the important and, for me, exciting task of "taking the bonds to market." This meant I would be a part of the team seeking a favorable rating for our Tower of the Americas revenue bonds from the official Wall Street rating agencies. I traveled to New York, accompanied by key staff in the city's finance department, our bond attorneys, and financial consultants. We met with bond-rating agencies, including Moody's and Standard and Poor's. We discussed the support that the business community and local citizens were giving the project and answered general questions about the city, and we received an excellent rating. The bonds were sold at 3.8 percent, a very low interest rate at the time.

～

I also supported the effort to develop the Women's Pavilion at the fair; a committee formed, chaired initially by Mrs. Harry Meyer (Willie) and later by Mrs. Winfield Hamlin (Vivian), who led the San Antonio Conservation Society for many years. To raise money for the pavilion, a fundraising luncheon was held in Washington, with the legendary party giver Perle Mesta as the official hostess. I was seated at the head table next to Vice President Hubert Humphrey's sister, who kept referring to me as the mayor's wife. She did not seem to understand that I

was a city councilwoman. At that time, there were
not many women serving as elected officials.

HemisFair planning also took me to Las Vegas,
where a new state-of-the-art convention center was
worth studying as we planned to build one as part of
the fair. On the airplane I was seated next to Mayor
Mac, who was known to be a very good card player.
He asked if I would like to play gin rummy, and I said
I'd be happy to play if we weren't playing for money.
He agreed but obviously thought it would be a tame
game. Never before in my life had I had such a string
of good luck as I had during that game. Every hand
worked perfectly, and I was calling out "gin" after
every two or three plays. At first Mayor Mac was
amused at my beginner's luck, but as I continued to
win, his countenance changed. Finally he stood and
yelled, "Get this female Red Berry off my hands!"
At that time Red Berry was a colorful San Antonio
personality who had been elected a state senator and
who, reportedly, was a known gambler.

In some ways HemisFair was a giant gamble for
San Antonio. The city council needed voter approval
for a $30 million general obligation bond issue to
fund the construction of the convention facilities and
to cover our share of urban renewal costs associated
with land purchases for the fair's footprint. As costs

were refined, the price tag for the convention facilities, which included a theater for the performing arts, an arena, and an exhibition building, exceeded the $8 million authorized by the bond issue. Jack Shelley, our city manager, had to get creative to come up with more than $3 million in additional funding. He recommended that we borrow the money from the sewer revenue bonds, and the city council authorized this so we could move ahead with construction. Some citizens and local media criticized the maneuver, but we knew the exhibition and performing spaces were essential to HemisFair's success, and we were running out of time. I think that in the ensuing years, San Antonio's expanding convention business, tourism, and reputation as a major international city have more than justified our decision.

As construction of the convention center progressed, there was a great deal of citizen interest. One day a delegation of prominent women came to my office, led by Margaret "Mag" Tobin, one of the city's best-known civic leaders and a patron of the arts. My visitors told me they had seen the interior hallways of the new arena, which was nearing completion, and that they were exceptionally unattractive. They told me that the color and pattern of the tiles were hideous and they needed to be removed and replaced immediately. When I saw the tile, I had to agree with them. The installation had a subway-tile checkerboard look, a combination of brown and cream. I told the mayor and city manager about the women's criticism and asked what would be involved in making a change. Mayor Mac decided to have a look himself, and he agreed that the checkerboard pattern was not too pleasing. The city manager said it would be too costly to remove all of the tile; he suggested we could pull out some of the brown tiles and create a random color accent, improving the look at a moderate cost. And that is what we did.

As preparations for HemisFair moved rapidly ahead, some controversy developed over the urban renewal plan. The architects wanted to restore and use some of the private homes and businesses that had been purchased, but they wanted to demolish others to produce a site plan that would accommodate all the pavilions and exhibit structures that the fair would need. The San Antonio Conservation Society and Sen. Ralph Yarborough became involved in a movement to protect many potentially historic sites, suggesting that a large number of those properties be saved and utilized in the HemisFair development plan. There were many meetings and negotiations to determine how many houses and buildings would be incorporated into the plans. Bexar County Historical Commission records indicate that twenty-four structures in HemisFair Park were designated as local landmarks.

As busy as city government and agencies were in making HemisFair a reality, San Antonio's private sector was working equally hard. Bill Sinkin was the first president of HemisFair corporation, with early backing from Congressman Henry B. González. When Bill stepped down for health reasons, Marshall Steves assumed the presidency, assembling a stellar executive committee that successfully raised the private underwriting needed from local businesses. Bill Sinkin became vice-chairman of the HemisFair board.

At the state level, Gov. John Connally was an ardent supporter of HemisFair, and at the national level, Sen. John Tower partnered with Congressman González to produce bipartisan authorization and funding.

H.B. "Pat" Zachry, CEO of the huge Zachry Construction Company, was the chairman of the executive committee. With his leadership and background in the construction business, he was able to overcome a myriad of obstacles to meet the fast-approaching deadline of April 6, 1968. At times, in the year pre-

Early advocates of the HemisFair project, including (*left to right*) Texas governor John Connally, H. B. "Pat" Zachry, Frank Manuppelli, and Mayor Walter McAllister, traveled to New York to promote it.

ceding HemisFair, we weren't certain we would open the gates on time.

~

As construction of the convention center progressed, there was discussion about eliminating the lower floor of the theater for the performing arts to save around $60,000. That floor, at river level, had rooms with windows that looked out at the turning basin for river barges. I felt this would be a big mistake. The lower-level rooms would provide needed space for rehearsals and receptions for special events, as well as flexibility for future needs. I succeeded in keeping the lower floors in the approved plans. Years later the theater for the performing arts was renamed the Lila Cockrell Theater, and my eightieth birthday party took place on that lower floor, hosted by my good friend Rosemary Kowalski, chair of the board of the RK Group, one of our nation's most successful catering and events–planning companies. Rosemary and I met during those planning days for HemisFair, when the city council selected Rosemary's small catering business to operate food concessions for the pavilions at the fair.

In 1966 a number of significant works of art were announced as gifts to enhance the new convention center and other sites of the fairgrounds, and the commissioned artists were busy creating them for the opening of the fair. The exterior facade of the theater for the performing arts would be covered by the largest mosaic mural in the country, created by Juan O'Gorman, a well-known Mexican artist and architect. A gift from Flora Cameron Kampmann (now Crichton), the *Confluence of Civilizations* would be a 25,000-square-foot mosaic of natural stones depicting diverse cultures living and working in harmony. O'Gorman used twelve stone colors in all; the blue stones are the only ones that did not come from Mexico.

~

Across the lagoon, the two-story stairwell of the convention center would become the site for a glass-tiled mural by Guatemalan artist Carlos Mérida, a contemporary interpretation of the fair's theme, given by Nancy Negley and the Brown Foundation in Houston. Almost fifty years later, when a remodeled and expanded convention center replaced the original, the mural was preserved and became the centerpiece of the beautiful new plaza at river level. A third mural was planned for inside the arena, spanning the interior entrances. Created by artist Fred Samuelson in acrylic on canvas, it too was preserved during later renovations and reinstalled in Ballroom C of the new center.

A sculpture by renowned artist David Smith, a gift from Ambassador and Mrs. Henry Catto, would be dramatically placed in the south end of the convention center lagoon. After the fair was over, however, a city public works crew on cleanup duty failed to recognize the sculpture as a major work of art and hauled it off to be converted to scrap metal. This was an extremely embarrassing moment for city officials, and a loss for our city. Later Jessica and Henry Catto had the sculpture reproduced, and it is part of the beautiful grounds of the McNay Art Museum. Other civic-minded donors made additional gifts of art, fountains, and other amenities. It was a true community effort.

In spring 1967, just one year before HemisFair's grand opening, as building construction and the creation of artworks progressed, another council election would take place. Gearing up for the election, I planted trees at the San Antonio Garden Center on Arbor Day, traveled to Mexico City with Sid for a Medical Society meeting, presented a city proclamation to the Pan American Optimist Club at their Salute to HemisFair event, and hosted a coffee in my home for my Tri Delta sorority honoring Hallie Spice as outstanding member of the year. Hallie was serving as the first woman president of the Fiesta San Antonio Commission and was past president of the Battle of Flowers Association, the Monte Vista Garden Club, and the Women of Saint Mark's Episcopal Church and was a life member of the Santa Rosa Children's Hospital Auxiliary. I spoke at the Women's Breakfast Club luncheon in observance of Texas Pioneer Day and addressed the National Council of Jewish Women at their annual community services luncheon.

Both local newspapers, the *San Antonio Light* and the *San Antonio Express-News*, photographed the GGL slate of incumbent council members as we registered for reelection in the city clerk's office. The election was scheduled for April 4, and we all knew that this year there would be competition for the seats we held. I hit the campaign trail with my colleagues, and as always the GGL took care of the bookings for our team. Other activities were sandwiched in between campaign events. I welcomed a delegation of visitors from Guadalajara, talked about trees for the southern boundary of HemisFair with Al Groves, consulting engineer for the Urban Renewal Agency, and wielded a shovel—still wearing my hat and gloves—at the ground breaking for the Austin Arms apartment complex being developed by Ray Ellison and Pat Legan.

～

Election day brought victory for six on the GGL team, but three of our group faced runoffs. When the runoff election was held, Roland Bremer was defeated by a young attorney, Pete Torres. This was the first loss for the GGL, and we wondered if it was a sign of bigger changes to come. I was happy to win an easy victory and was looking forward to my next term and to welcoming a world of visitors to HemisFair 1968.

But first I welcomed family and friends at Southwestern University in May, when Carol graduated with honors. I marveled at the fact that our firstborn child was now a college graduate. Summertime saw each member of our family going in a different direction. Carol had a summer job at Frost Bank, Cathy took a summer course at San Antonio College, Sid journeyed to Atlantic City for the annual meeting of the American Medical Association, and I went to Boston for the annual conference of the National League of Cities. Then, along with Mayor Mac and several other council members, I joined a postconference tour to Montreal to see Expo 67. The Montreal Expo was a much larger international exposition than HemisFair would be, but the visit gave us important ideas for how we might improve our model for visitor relations and hospitality.

I experienced more hospitality firsthand when I visited Cape Canaveral at the invitation of San

Antonio's military community. Our group included Mayor Mac, mayor pro tem Jack Gatti, council members Dr. Herbert Calderón, Bob Jones, Dr. Gerald Parker, and the Rev. S. H. James, as well as county commissioner Ollie Wurzbach, state senator Frank Lombardino, and others. The fascinating trip included a briefing on the development of the Saturn rocket designed to carry our spacecraft into orbit. It would be the launch vehicle for the Apollo moon program, flying twenty-four humans to the moon between 1969 and 1972.

∼

Back in Texas, the fall season was busy. Carol began teaching at Longfellow Junior School, in the San Antonio Independent School system, and the *San Antonio Light* published an article highlighting her ideas, to illustrate what new teachers were experiencing. Cathy was back at TCU majoring in elementary education and participating in extracurricular activities. I was named by SMU as one of six women to receive the university's Women of Achievement award. Willis M. Tate, SMU's president, presented each honoree with a silver bowl at a luncheon during homecoming week. I was especially honored that,

In preparation for HemisFair, the San Antonio River was
diverted to create a new entry to the buildings under construction. Congressman Henry B. González and I cut the
celebratory ribbon to open the waterway.

in addition to family members, Mayor McAllister
attended the ceremonies.

As 1967 drew to a close, the river extension connecting the existing river bend to the HemisFair area
was completed. Congressman González and I cut

the ribbon for the extension, proud of the entrance it created to the convention center and its various facilities. The river was aglow with thousands of sparkling lights, the Christmas tree in Alamo Plaza was spectacular, and the city's citizens felt the magic of downtown during the holidays. I knew more magic was just a little more than three months away, and I prayed we would be ready for our upcoming international fair. Thirty-one countries were participating, and millions were counting on us.

The Tower of the Americas was a subject of great interest to everyone in the city. Designed by architect Boone Powell, it was an almost continuous concrete pour, from the ground up, for the vertical pedestal, which contained three elevator shafts, the staircase, and space for the electrical and plumbing service facilities. The top house, a circular structure with three levels—the restaurant level, a lounge and bar level, and the observation level—was built on the ground and lifted up to a perch by crane. On the day of the tower's ascension, all went well as the top house began its journey. About a third of the way up, one of the cables broke. The top house lifting was stalled, and it was left hanging at a slightly tilted angle for several weeks while there was a search for a heavier crane and cables. Finally the new equipment arrived, and the job was completed, to everyone's relief.

When the tower was nearing completion and the final touches were being made to the top house, Mayor McAllister decided the city council should ride the construction elevator to the top of the tower to see how everything looked from above. When we arrived at the site, several workmen told the mayor it was considered unlucky for a woman to ride in an elevator before a structure was completed and open to the public. Mayor Mac turned a deaf ear to their comments, grabbed my arm, and said, "Lila is going!" Quite frankly I would have been happy to accommodate the workmen's wishes, but I dutifully followed the mayor and other council members into the elevator. About halfway up, it abruptly stopped. I wondered if everyone was thinking it was my fault for being aboard. A television crew was accompanying us, and the cameraman filmed us while we were waiting—and hoping!—for the ascent to resume. I quipped, "Well, if we are going to be on television, I will try to look brave." That evening I heard my remark quoted on the news. Luckily, to our great relief, after a very long fifteen minutes our journey to the top of the tower continued.

While Pat Zachry worked frenetically with his

executive committee to complete final arrangements, he was rushing as head of Zachry Construction to get the Hilton Palacio del Rio hotel finished. The need for additional first-class hotel rooms down-town had been obvious immediately, and Mr. Pat had stepped up to the plate. Southwest Research Institute had developed a unique fast-track method of construction for Zachry. The hotel's foundation and central vertical core, elevator shafts and utility lines included, were constructed on-site. Individual hotel rooms were constructed off-site. The concrete shells were created in one location and moved to a second location to be furnished. The finished rooms were brought to the hotel site and hoisted by crane, one by one, into place. This approach attracted a lot of attention in San Antonio and beyond, making international news as an innovative engineering and construction process. Our citizens watched with amazement as the hotel took shape during those countdown days before the fair's opening.

~

Construction for HemisFair was our city's main focus in early 1968, but the opening of the new San Antonio Public Library marked a major milestone too. Located on the corner of Saint Mary's and Market

Streets, the library provided much-needed space for expanding collections and was strong evidence that the city valued literacy and learning. As with most projects, some behind-the-scene dramas challenged the project in its early days. When planning began, a first step was selection of the architect. Mayor Mac had a candidate in mind—Ben Wyatt. Most of the other council members wanted to select Phil Carrington, another local architect who built many San Antonio residences in the 1960s. The debate caused some friction, so to move things along, Mayor Mac decided to hire both architects and to instruct them to work together on the design. This did not work out well, since their architectural styles were quite different. The council looked at plans A, B, C, D, E, and F without approving any of them. About this time Mayor Mac departed with his wife on a long-planned trip to Europe. While he was gone, plan G was developed, mostly by Phil Carrington, then quickly approved and moved into implementation. When the mayor returned, we told him he would be pleased to know the council had finally made a decision and that the library project was under way.

The days flew by as April—and HemisFair—approached. Sid and I were invited to be part of the small group inside one of the finished hotel rooms being hoisted by crane to complete the Hilton Palacio del Rio. I was a little apprehensive as the crane lifted us up and gently slipped us into the nesting place for the last room. The result was a wonderful hotel, with a beautifully decorated ballroom and private function spaces, across the street from the convention center. Everything was in place for the grand opening of HemisFair.

~

Invitations to functions and receptions arrived with every mail delivery. Excitement was building. Then, almost on the eve of the opening, a national tragedy occurred. On April 4, 1968, the Rev. Martin Luther King was assassinated in Memphis. He was the country's most prominent and charismatic leader in the civil rights movement, and his murder created an immediate outpouring of outrage and grief. There were rumors of demonstrations that might take place across the country, including at HemisFair. President and Mrs. Lyndon Johnson had been scheduled to attend the opening ceremonies, but the president decided to remain in Washington to try to bring calm to the nation and to show full respect for the situation. Lady Bird Johnson did attend for the opening festivities, however, accompanied by

Henry B. González, Lady Bird Johnson, and Walter McAllister joined other national and international dignitaries on the opening day of HemisFair '68.

the secretary of the interior, Stewart Udall. Gov. and Mrs. John Connally were also in attendance, along with many other international, national, state, and local officials.

The festivities began on the evening of April 5 with a reception at the Ford Pavilion, followed by a reception hosted by the Connallys at the Texas Pavilion, which had been built as a permanent structure that would continue as the Institute of Texan Cultures long after the fair ended. The next day HemisFair opened to the public. Pavilion openings and ceremonial events with honored guests and attendees moving through the ninety-seven-acre site continued all day. The Women's Pavilion, which so many local women leaders had worked hard to create, opened in midafternoon with local dynamos Patsy Steves and Edith McAllister greeting guests. In the late afternoon those attending the evening black-tie event at the theater for the performing arts scurried home or to their hotels to change into formal attire. They returned for a special performance of the opera *Don Carlo*, which had been underwritten by Margaret "Mag" Tobin and her son Robert Tobin and was to be the spectacular finale to opening day. Because it was a rather long opera, the plan was to open with the first act and then recess in the theater lobby for an intermission with an elegant buffet dinner catered by Rosemary Kowalski's company.

The dinner was accompanied by a lovely wine service, and guests enjoyed the relaxed interlude. After dinner everyone returned to their seats for the second act. It was not long before the official openings and activities of the strenuous day, combined with the delicious dinner and wine, began to take their toll on the guests. Shortly after the lights were dimmed and the opera resumed, heads began to nod. Sid and I were seated a short distance behind the First Lady and Secretary Udall, and we observed that they were making a valiant effort to remain alert and attentive, as were other guests. By the beginning of the third act, however, the audience had dwindled until the theater was only half full. Finally my beloved spouse whispered in my ear that we too were slipping out, and I did not try to convince him otherwise.

From opening day until its closing in October, HemisFair was San Antonio's civic focus, and activities continued nonstop. Behind the scenes the executive committee was staying on top of the revenues and expenses. However, this became increasingly stressful for the executive committee because attendance figures were not reaching the projected levels. At the same time, payrolls had to be met and some contractors were still waiting for payment on some of the last construction costs. Those who attended the fair seemed delighted with it, and attendance rose in the last few months, but it was hard to make up for the slow start.

Adding to that disappointment, an unfortunate misunderstanding had developed between two of the city's most influential leaders, both major champions of HemisFair. When H. B. "Pat" Zachry stepped up to meet the need for more downtown hotel rooms and constructed the Hilton Palacio del Rio hotel, he also saw the need for a parking garage near the hotel. It needed to be large enough to accommodate both hotel guests and visitor parking for fair attendees who lived in San Antonio.

According to reports that circulated at the time, Mayor Mac had urged Mr. Pat to construct the parking garage. He agreed to ask the city to purchase and operate it as a city public garage, probably intending to use revenue bonds to finance the purchase. Due to time constraints and the need to expedite the construction schedule, overtime and other costs came into play. The final construction cost of the high-rise parking garage was much higher than Mayor Mac had expected. I was not party to any of the discussions that ensued and can only report what I've been told, but the bottom line was that Mayor Mac declined to move ahead with the city's purchase. This became an unresolved dispute that left some of us on the city council feeling uncomfortable. I was personally thankful when, some years later, City Public Service (CPS) agreed to purchase the parking garage and add an additional two floors for office space.

When HemisFair closed in October, everyone who had worked so hard on San Antonio's big dream was tired. But there was still a lot to be done. A final accounting needed to be completed, some exhibition buildings would be closed and others would be repurposed, and careful planning for the reuse of the fairgrounds needed to be considered. While the fair did not generate the projected revenues or visitor count in 1968, it transformed San Antonio and empowered it to attract the booming national and international convention business that would ensure its future as a major city in the United States.

EIGHT

A Ladylike Strategy

1969–74

After a busy campaign in 1969, orchestrated once more by the GGL, I was reelected to the city council for a fourth term. Not every candidate on our slate was elected, however, as the GGL lost a second seat in 1969. We all sensed a subtle change under way in city government. Walter McAllister was elected mayor for the fifth time, and I was elected mayor pro tem by vote of the city council. This was the first time a woman had held the position, and I was thrilled. With the election behind us, we settled down to work.

～

During my years on the council, I had discovered an effective way to be an agent for change in the city. I realized that council members had a lot of power in appointing the boards of municipal agencies, and I knew those appointments were important. In many ways, these boards controlled the development of the city. They included the City Public Service Board, the boards of the San Antonio Development Agency and Zoning Commission, the water board, the planning commission board, and the board of City Transit, which is now VIA Metropolitan Transit. Anglo men dominated the scene on all of the boards and their committees. From my first days at the city council table, I tried to get more women and minorities on the boards. I researched which positions were open and arrived with a list of qualified women to put forward. Sometimes my fellow council members, especially John Gatti, would say, "Oh, Lila, do we have to?" And I would say, "Yes, you have to. I don't have anything against Anglo men—I am married to one. But we need opportunities for women and minorities." John Gatti just chuckled. We would joke about it, but he knew I meant business.

I always studied upcoming vacancies and researched my candidates. I never brought forward a name just to have a woman or an African American or a Hispanic selected. My candidates always had every qualification. They were not always appointed, but I did open some initial doors, and I got the first woman appointed to the City Transit board. I tried

to get Irene Wischer, president of Panhandle Producing Company, appointed to the City Public Service
Board but was unsuccessful. Her background in the
oil and gas business made her a perfect candidate for a
utility board, but that was the top appointment in the
city. It would be another six years before a woman
held that position.

Change was slow in coming, but it was happening.
It was exciting to see the Mayor's Commission on
the Status of Women established during Mayor Mac's
last term. I worked on the preliminary planning with
a group of highly gifted women, including Lynette
Glasscock and Irene Wischer, and we were confident
that the commission would have a huge impact on
the future of San Antonio.

~

I believe one reason I got things done is that I did not
come to the table with a shrill voice. I never forgot
that I was a southern lady, and I always tried to deal
with people in a ladylike—but firm—way. Everyone
knew I was serious, but I did not scream at them or
berate them. I said, "This is something that is right,
and we must do it."

Mayor McAllister also had a special style for
getting things done. He was forceful in getting his

"Mayor Mac" (*right*) was the first person to encourage me to run for public office. I served with him in city government for eight years, and he was a dynamo—whether leading our city, meeting with celebrities like Lawrence Welk (*left*), or fishing on the Texas coast.

points across but was a charming gentleman in many ways. I remember disagreeing on an issue concerning public housing and being invited to his office for a little chat. His secretary made tea and served us cupcakes, and as we enjoyed our tea party, he said, "I wanted to explain to you my views on the issue." Mayor Mac felt that we already had enough public housing and did not need to seek federal funding. But I felt that there were so many people living in substandard, unhealthy conditions that we should not pass up the opportunity for federal help to increase our supply of subsidized housing. We had a lovely visit, and he was gracious, courtly, and gentlemanly, but I was not persuaded to change my position. I think he was disappointed. He had made the effort to convince me with great style, and I appreciated that.

Mayor McAllister served ten years as mayor, and I served with him for eight of them. He is the person who encouraged me to become an elected official, and I learned a lot from him. I also enjoyed working with John Gatti and thought he was very smart, with a strong background in municipal finance. He was much more liberal in his viewpoints than Mayor Mac, but he was always respectful and was able to get a lot done because he got along so well with the mayor.

It was the GGL strategy for a retiring council member to step down before the end of the term, allowing his or her replacement to serve by appointment before becoming the candidate in the next election. As I prepared to leave office in 1970, Carol Haberman was chosen to take my place. She was an attorney and active in the Business and Professional

Women's group and other women's organizations. She was very visible in the community. She was appointed to fill my unexpired term so that she could run in 1971 as an incumbent.

As my days on the city council were ending, Cathy's days as a college student were coming to an end too. Before graduation, she had applied to be a flight attendant for American Airlines and had been hired, and she went almost directly to work. With her roommate, another flight attendant, she took advantage of the privileges of her job to travel to Europe and other places, and Sid and I benefited as well. We traveled to Hawaii as her guests; then Cathy flew on to Fiji. Standing in the Honolulu airport, watching my daughter fly away, I felt trepidation because her destination sounded so far away and I would not be there to look after her. I grappled with a mother's protective feelings. She waved, and I realized that she was a grown woman, on her own.

That summer, after I left the council, my mother invited me to accompany her on a six-week trip to Europe, sponsored by the *Christian Herald*. I had never been to Europe, and our adventure included stops in England, Ireland, Holland, and Germany, where we saw a passion play that is only presented every ten years, in Oberammergau.

~

When I returned to Texas, I went to work and found it was not nearly as stressful as serving on the council. I worked briefly as the part-time community relations director for the Ecumenical Center for Religion and Health. After a few months I saw an ad for a full-time community relations position at what was then the San Antonio Tuberculosis Hospital. Not much progress had been made in the treatment of the disease, and patients still faced long hospital stays with lots of bed rest and medication. Even when no longer infectious, patients endured a lengthy recuperation and often grew bored and depressed. I developed programs for the patients, partnering with community groups like the Rotary Club, the Kiwanis Club, and the Lions Club to bring speakers, entertainment, and other events to the hospital. Many of the service groups were located on the South Side, and I met many leaders from that part of San Antonio and learned more about our city from the experience.

I was enjoying my work, until the GGL contacted me in 1973. Once again I heard the irresistible siren call of the city council. As expected, Carol Haberman had been elected for the 1971–73 term, but instead of running for reelection, she decided to run for a county court at law judgeship. At that time women judges were scarce, and I admit I was nervous because three women were running for judgeships in county courts at law that year. I was worried that too many women were trying to land positions at the same time. To everyone's surprise, and my delight, all three women, including Carol Haberman, were elected.

When the GGL learned that Carol Haberman would not be running for reelection to the council, they asked me to return as a candidate. Adding me to the ticket would be quick and easy, and I agreed. An internal split was occurring within the GGL, however, over the mayoral position. The GGL placed Roy Barrera, a well-known Hispanic civic leader and criminal lawyer, on the ticket. When Charles Becker was not chosen as the candidate, he broke with the GGL and filed as an opposition candidate, launching a strong negative attack on Roy Barrera. At that time the city council—not the citizens of San Antonio— selected the mayor, and Charles Becker was able to get enough votes from the independents on the council to win the election. He served from 1973 until 1975, and I joined Dr. José San Martín, the Rev. Claude Black, Glenn Lacy, Clifford Morton, Alfred

In 1973 I returned to the city council, still the only woman, and served with (*left to right*) Alfred Beckmann, Cliff Morton, Glenn Lacy, Claude Black, Mayor Charles Becker, Dr. José San Martín, Leo Mendoza, and Alvin Padilla Jr.

G. Beckmann, Dr. D. Ford Nielsen, Alvin G. Padilla Jr., and Leo Mendoza Jr. on the council.

Mayor Becker was an interesting personality. He was from a prominent family that owned Handy Andy, a large grocery corporation at the time. He had grown up as part of the social establishment in San Antonio, and yet he was antiestablishment and did not care for anyone who followed traditional social patterns. I would call him a maverick.

I remember one council meeting when he called us to order and talked for an hour about the movie

The Towering Inferno, which he had seen the night before. He went on and on about it. Suddenly I got it. That night the annual meeting of the Greater San Antonio Chamber of Commerce had taken place. He wanted everyone to know he had gone to the movies and not to the dinner.

Mayor Becker was fond of a little Italian restaurant on the West Side near the Mercado area. It was a casual place with very good Italian food. He would insist that the whole council go there for lunch. In the past we had eaten a light catered meal at city hall, which did not take much time. Now we went to the Italian restaurant. The waiters would offer wine with the meal, and we were always late getting back. The council meeting was supposed to begin at 1 p.m. but never got going before 1:30. Those who had enjoyed perhaps two glasses of wine were quite relaxed, and our afternoon session had a different tone than the morning meeting. Perhaps it was a result of my pro-hibitionist grandfather or my love of punctuality, but I found these lunches slightly worrisome.

I was far more worried, however, about energy problems that I feared were looming for the city and urged the council to be watchful. San Antonio had a twenty-year contract with Coastal States Gas and its subsidiary, the LoVaca Gathering Company, to provide our natural gas at the set price of about twenty-five cents per 1,000 cubic feet. But LoVaca did not have the reserves it had claimed; they had to purchase their gas at a higher price, and the increased cost was passed through to its buyers, including San Antonio. Consumers' energy bills increased ten-fold, and I felt we should sue Coastal States for breach of contract. Mayor Becker did not agree; he felt the company was run by great people and that its owner, Oscar Wyatt, was a smart man.

I kept saying that, as representatives of our taxpayers, who are also our ratepayers, we needed to sue Coastal States. The situation started to escalate, and I began to emerge as a spokesperson within the GGL on the issue.

But the GGL no longer automatically ruled the city council, because it no longer had all the elected positions of the council, as it had in the past. There was a five-to-four split at the time, with the independents in the majority. Right after Charles Becker was elected mayor, I proposed we elect Dr. José San Martín as the mayor pro tem, thinking that as part of the GGL he would be a helpful balance since the mayor was an independent. Instead Mayor Becker suggested we adopt a new rotating system for mayor pro tem, where each council member served for a short term, six weeks or so. When it was time to vote, the Rev. Claude Black did not vote with the rest of the GGL group. He felt that the rotating system would provide the opportunity for an African American to be in the position of mayor pro tem for the first time. That was very important to him, so he supported Mayor Becker's idea.

Reverend Black was a very active East Side community leader who had appeared before the council often in the past. He was intelligent and affable, but he never lost sight of his mission to ensure opportunities for African Americans to be recognized and included in decision making. I think it is important to remember that, unlike many other cities, San Antonio's African American population is relatively small, running at about 6.5 to 7 percent of the total population. This has always been a factor in that community's participation level in city government. But Reverend Black and his mentor, G. J. Sutton, were powerful advocates for change and always presented the issues of their community effectively. When Reverend Black left the GGL group to vote with the independents, I realized that the GGL was over.

∾

It was during this time that we first began hearing from Communities Organized for Public Service

(COPS). Ernie Cortés, who had trained under Saul Alinsky, the Chicago-based author of *Rules for Radicals* and the founder of modern community organizing, established COPS to drive an agenda of issues of importance to the San Antonio neighborhoods, especially those of the West Side, which were predominantly Hispanic. To get their agenda items through, the group embraced what they called pressure methods, believing those tactics were necessary for their success. I did not like those methods, because they did not encourage coming in, sitting down, and trying to negotiate. COPS became a large group trying to intimidate leadership into taking a particular course of action. They held "COPS accountability meetings," which council members and candidates were invited to. We were given lectures, followed by presentation of COPS plans and lists of what they wanted funded. While this political strategy differed from mine, I realized that the COPS constituency was making its needs and aspirations known, something that had not really happened before.

I remember a big public meeting COPS staged in a West Side church, with all the city council candidates in attendance. COPS had developed an agenda of $100 million in projects they wanted. Many were very good projects, but they were only in certain areas of the city where COPS wielded influence. That night COPS leaders called on each candidate and asked, "Will you support our list of $100 million of improvements?" Every person said yes, and then it was my turn. "Let me just say that the list you have would require different ways of funding," I said. At this point I was interrupted, before I could explain that some would need to be funded under community development grants and other ways.

When the city council prepares a bond election, it usually includes projects all over the city, East and West Sides, Center City, South Side, and North Side. Before I could explain that, the COPS leaders said, "No, we did not ask you that. Yes or no, will you support these projects on the bond issue?" I responded, "If either yes or no is the only way I can answer, then the answer is no." I am the only one who said that.

COPS used a group-style leadership model instead of identifying one spokesperson. But Catholic priests were perhaps the closest to being in charge, and Father Albert Benavides often presented the group's views at city council, berating us for many things. I had received some literature that COPS was distributing in Houston, where they were in the early stages of organizing. The Houston pamphlet described the marvelous successes they had brought about in San Antonio. At one of the many protests Father Benavides organized at city hall, I quoted his words from the pamphlet, where he praised the city council for its assistance. He was amused but did not want to show it. Trying hard not to laugh, all of us continued the meeting on a less contentious note. There was a mellowing, and over the years I supported many of the initiatives that COPS introduced. My loyalty has always been to our city as a whole.

~

In fall 1974, Mexico's president, Luis Echeverría, initiated an international trade fair to be held in San Antonio for three years. Knowing that the event would take place again the following year, I took a delegation of about twenty-five San Antonio business leaders to Mexico to present a formal invitation to President Echeverría to personally open the fair. Before I went, I received a briefing and was told that the president was not always cordial to *norteamericanos* and that I probably would not get an answer, just a promise to take the invitation under advisement. Our delegation, which included banker Tom Frost, civic leaders Bill and Faye Sinkin, and others, went to Los Pinos to see the president. I took a painting of the

When I visited President Luis Echeverría in Mexico, I gave him a painting of the San Antonio River to encourage him to attend the opening of an international trade fair in San Antonio.

San Antonio River as a gift and told him we would be thrilled if he would come to our city. When I presented him with the painting, he had a painting taken down from his office wall and gave it to me. After our exchange of gifts, he agreed to come to San Antonio for the 1975 fair.

The president asked when our delegation was returning to Texas, and I told him we would depart the next day. He asked if those plans were firm; I was not sure what to say. He extended an invitation to our group to fly to Cancún to see the newest resort, El Presidente Hotel, which was about to have its grand opening. He wanted us to see how wonderful it was and to tell everyone at home about it. I huddled with the delegation, and everyone except Tom Frost, who had a bank board meeting in San Antonio, was able to stay a little longer.

The next day we were transported from our hotel to the president's personal airplane. We flew to Cancún, where we were welcomed by a hostess from the new hotel. As we were driving to our destination, she told me she had received a telephone call from the president at midnight to say that he was sending twenty-five dear friends to the hotel the next day. She said the hotel was fully booked for the night, but the staff had performed a miracle. I don't know who got kicked out for the president's dear friends, but we had a wonderful time and flew from Cancún to San Antonio the next day on the president's plane. When we arrived at customs, officials asked with astonishment, "Is that the president of Mexico's plane?" The next year, after I became mayor, President Echeverría did come to San Antonio, staying for three days at the Hilton.

~

In fall 1974, people began to approach me about
running for mayor the following year. I was hesi-
tant—could a woman really be elected? But I was
encouraged by the recent election of Carol Haberman and two other women to judge positions, and I
began to consider it. By now the GGL had splintered
into three factions and was considering three possible
mayoral candidates: Dr. José San Martín, John Steen,
and myself.

Dr. San Martín was a strong leader of a Mexican
American group—a separate coalition called the
Westside Preservation Alliance—that had long been
affiliated with the GGL. He had been very active and
had the support of many Hispanic leaders who felt it
was time for a Hispanic to run for mayor. We were
friends and had worked well together on the council when Charles Becker was mayor. He had been
hopeful of being mayor pro tem then, but it did not
happen. Now he wanted to run for mayor and had a
strong group of supporters. He said that if I became
a candidate, however, he would not run against me,
because we had worked so well together.

John Steen also had a group of GGL backers, and
he was more typical of the organization's traditional

For the first time in San Antonio's history, the mayor would be elected by the voters at large. I became the first woman to run for that office.

values. He was an affluent business leader, like many of the other mayoral candidates GGL chose, and he had the added advantage of having once chaired the organization.

I knew that discussions were going on within the GGL about favorite candidates. I never campaigned to be selected, never asked anyone to fight for my candidacy. Eventually the GGL approached me and said that, after much thought, they had decided to invite me to be their mayoral candidate in the 1975 election. I was the first woman they had sponsored for mayor.

I would run under a new set of rules. In the past the mayor had been selected by a majority vote of the city council. But in November 1974 San Antonio voters passed a charter amendment to hold a direct election of the mayor by all voters.

I never was active in a political party; I always have voted for the person or the issue. I usually voted in Republican primaries, but I had never taken any political office within that party and had always voted for candidates from both parties in the general election. I never made my thinking public about national issues, but I did take public stands on city and local issues. My early experience with the nonpartisan League of Women Voters had prepared me well. I had no trouble being good friends with Sen. John Tower, a Republican, and with Rep. Henry B. González, a Democrat. My loyalties have always been to all the citizens of San Antonio, and that was the bedrock of my mayoral campaign.

I ran against a formidable slate, and it was a challenging race. Eloy Centeno, owner of a well-known grocery chain, with many stores on the West Side, was a strong candidate. John Monfrey was another prominent opponent. He was the distributor of Falstaff beer, and his signs were in bars all over town. He presented himself as a "man's man" and had an active group of supporters. There was a sea of yard signs around town displaying his name and picture. He and I ended up in a runoff, which was hard fought—nothing like those early days when the GGL had been able to deliver an election easily.

The 1975 election was the GGL's last gasp. In addition to my election as mayor, it won only two council seats, with the election of the Rev. Claude Black and a young twenty-seven-year-old named Henry G. Cisneros. The Independent Team—which was a strange name since independents don't usually run as a team—won six seats: Phil Pyndus, Robert P. "Bob" Billa, Glen Hartman, Al Rohde, Richard Teniente, and Dr. D. Ford Nielsen.

I remember some people saying that I would be mayor in name only because I did not have a GGL majority on the council. I did not pay any attention to that. I would follow the strategy I had always used. I would work with the council to build a good working coalition of people who wanted to see San Antonio move ahead. I knew we would face challenges together, but I was the one sitting in the mayor's seat. I had also been elected president of the Texas Municipal League, the first woman to serve in that capacity. I smiled at my new council members, exuding friendliness, happiness, and good thoughts about what lay ahead.

NINE

Madam Mayor

1975–81

I would often need to summon those tools—friend-liness, happiness, and good thoughts—to sustain me during the challenges of my eight-year adventure as mayor. There were some major battles, important changes, and wonderful successes for our city—and I am proud of them all.

Early in my first term, a new amendment to the Voting Rights Act of 1965 was being enforced throughout the country. The original law was designed to end racial discrimination in elections, and a decade later amendments were still being made to strengthen it. Some cities resisted, but San Antonio made the required changes, which included amending our city charter. Recognizing that our long-standing election of nine council members at large did not provide representation of our entire city, we decided to adopt a districting plan. There was some opposition, but most people felt that the move was better than the possibility of extended litigation with the federal government. The districting plan took several years to design and passed in January 1977, before the city election that spring.

In the meantime problems with the city's gas provider, Coastal States and LoVaca Gathering, continued to escalate, and consumer energy costs continued to soar. My earlier warnings as a councilwoman had been proven true. Mayor Becker had chosen not to sue Coastal States, but I was in the mayor's seat now and had to act on behalf of the citizens of San Antonio. As mayor, I also held a seat on the board of our utility company, the CPSB, the first woman to do so.

Before and during the lawsuit that ensued, the ongoing contentious negotiations between the parties were covered dramatically by the media. The City of San Antonio and City Public Service were represented by attorneys Wilbur Matthews, Jon Wood, and Roger Wilson; they also called on the expertise of several CPS board members who were in the energy business, including John E. Newman and Dr. Robert West. They held many meetings with the Coastal States CEO, Oscar Wyatt, and LoVaca Gathering Company's senior vice president, William E. Greehey.

As mayor, I held a seat on the CPS Energy board,
along with (*left to right*) Earl Hill, Eloy Centeno, Ruben
Escobedo, and Glenn Biggs.

I felt we were on our way to winning the lawsuit
when we were approached with plans for a settlement.
I told the City Public Service Board that I would not
agree to a settlement until they could tell me that we

had gotten everything we could possibly get if we chose to see the lawsuit through to the end. They felt we had a good deal, and our CPS attorneys came to see me and ask if I would agree to the settlement. I told them that in addition to the cash settlement, we needed one more thing.

I knew that part of the complex settlement agreement included the reorganization of LoVaca Gathering Company and that plans were to locate its new headquarters in Corpus Christi, Texas. I told the attorneys that we wanted the new company to be in San Antonio because we needed new industry. We had more customers here, and I thought we deserved it. The negotiating attorney for LoVaca responded that he could not do that. That's when I said, "Then I will see you in court!" He turned and walked out with a dejected look on his face.

Pretty soon I received word that in addition to receiving more than $100 million, we had an agreement that the reorganized company headquarters would be in San Antonio. That really was the biggest prize because the new company became Valero Energy, which has provided an extraordinary boost to our city's economy, is today a Fortune 500 company with assets of more than $44 billion, and is one of San Antonio's most philanthropic corporate citizens.

It also has spun off, or been responsible for creating, several new companies. I am happy that my firmness in the negotiations brought this business growth to our city.

Another hard-fought battle had to do with our coal contracts. During the energy crisis of the 1970s, we diversified our fuel sources to include gas, oil, coal, and nuclear, to avoid repeating the problem we had with Coastal States when our utility company depended solely on them. CPS Energy began to buy special "clean coal" that came from Wyoming, transported by the Burlington Northern Railroad. But by 1976 coal freight rates were rising almost monthly, and this was affecting our utility company's ability to deliver reliable, affordable power to our citizens.

The railroads were governed by the Interstate Commerce Commission, and Burlington Northern had powerful lobbyists in Washington who were able to establish a monopoly railroad route for their client and get the rate increases through. I began to make trips to Washington as well, determined to talk to every Congress member I could about the ICC. Finally, out of frustration I suggested that we sue Burlington Northern. Once again we were involved in a major lawsuit, and again we won a big judgment. Part of the settlement involved opening the railroad route from Gillette, Wyoming, to San Antonio to another carrier, Union Pacific. Once there was competition, the rates went down. Soon Union Pacific became our carrier for the coal that was delivered to San Antonio's power plants.

A third utility battle was over the South Texas Project. When we began diversifying our fuel sources, we partnered with several other cities to build the first nuclear power plant in Texas, near Baytown just outside of Houston. The idea was not popular. The capital costs of building a nuclear plant are high, but the cost of the fuel itself is low. I had been persuaded that in the long term, San Antonio would benefit from participating in the project. The original estimate to build the plant was about $1 billion, which turned out to be grossly under the actual cost. Houston-based construction company Brown & Root was the contractor, but it had never built a nuclear plant and the costs kept rising. Well-meaning citizens began attending every council meeting, urging us to get out of the South Texas Project. They said it was too expensive, and they also raised environmental concerns about nuclear energy. Arguments against the project were rising, and media attention fueled the debate. This was a difficult time, a time for some real soul-searching. As mayor, I worked to stay on

Best wishes to Lila Cockrell
Rosalynn Carter Jimmy Carter

I met President and Mrs. Jimmy Carter in Washington when San Antonio received a Model City award. I contacted the president again when I was working to end the railroad monopoly that demanded high costs to transport coal during the energy crisis of the 1970s.

A newspaper cartoon illustrated some of my more difficult "dancing partners" during San Antonio's energy crisis.

course, and eventually the plant was built for more than $5 billion. Over the years since it became operational, delivery costs for energy from the nuclear plant have been lower than from any of our other power sources. Today it provides 35 percent of San Antonio's energy. We did the right thing, but it was hard.

I call these my "energy wars"—the natural gas shortage, the coal delivery problem, and the nuclear power controversy. They happened on my watch, and they were important issues. I am grateful to all the people who worked with me, telling me the truth about the facts in each case. When I felt confident that the facts supported the positions I took, I stood my ground.

There were also some delightful times, especially those involving international relations. When President Echeverría came to San Antonio for the second trade fair, he brought a large entourage and stayed in town for three days. Following the opening ceremony, we took a grand tour of the exposition of Mexico's products. The president stopped at every exhibit booth, looked it over carefully, saw something he liked, and said, "I think Mayor Cockrell would like that." Then the item would be presented to me. This was a new experience for me, and I did not know what to do. I said thank you at each booth and handed each item to my staff. Soon we needed something to carry the growing number of items. My staff got a golf cart, and by the end of the tour, it was piled high with products from Mexico. We were not going to keep all these gifts, of course; we would need to find an appropriate place for them. But I did keep two items. One is a painting of some fruit, and the other is an area rug with an early Mexican cultural design.

The last booth on the tour was an exhibit of beautiful Mexican folk art. There were thirty pieces of exquisite work. I loved them all and said so. President Echeverría smiled and said, "It is yours." He gave me the entire collection, and I was thrilled to accept the gift on behalf of the citizens of San Antonio. The San Antonio Museum of Art was given most of the pieces, and others went to the Institute of Texan Cultures. I think the president wanted to make these gifts because he realized I truly appreciated his country and its work; because I was a woman, I could be openly exuberant and enthusiastic, and he could respond with generosity and friendship.

But President Echeverría also held his ground when confronted by anyone unfriendly. As he was leaving the trade fair after another visit, Mario Cantú, a well-known local restaurateur, accused the president of something and began haranguing him. In a flash the president gave the complainer a blow to the jaw and flattened him, right there on the street. That event didn't get into the newspapers, and the rest of the visit went smoothly.

∾

When I was elected, I became the mayor of the largest city with a woman at its helm. I held that distinction for four years, until Jane Byrne was elected mayor of Chicago. It opened doors for me at both the annual U.S. Conference of Mayors and the National League of Cities meetings. I was often asked to join important international delegations since it was important to include two or three women in the mix. I participated in the first mayors' trip to the People's Republic of China and was in the first group that traveled to Taiwan. I traveled to Germany to study culture and urban development, crossing what was then the Iron Curtain to tour Warsaw and Budapest.

I may have been the first San Antonio mayor active in national organizations like these. By participating, I met many federal officials who had a lot of clout when I went after federal grants. Because we knew each other, they were more willing to help. Occasionally one hears complaints about a mayor who travels and goes on international junkets. I think it is a mistake to believe that the mayor should stay in his or her city all the time. The amount of money it costs to participate is very small compared to the cost of running a city, and the benefits can be immense.

The Sister Cities International program is another important part of San Antonio; over the years our city has become sisters with eleven cities, but when I was mayor, there were only three. In Mexico, we had established strong ties with Guadalajara and Monterrey, and then we added Las Palmas in the Canary Islands. Later, under Henry Cisneros, Kumamoto, Japan, was added.

∼

I ran for reelection in 1977, and once again John Monfrey was my strongest opponent. It was a colorful election and the first one that required me to raise my own money to campaign. The GGL had always taken care of that, and it was not something I enjoyed—so I ran a low-budget campaign. I called a press conference and issued a challenge to my opponent—to meet me at city hall at high noon on a certain date to debate the major issues facing the city. He did not come, so we staged the debate without him. My team put two chairs in front of the steps at city hall. One had his name on it, and the other had mine. The day of the debate, Mr. Monfrey's campaign team published a glossy newspaper brochure describing how wonderful he would be for San Antonio, claiming it took a businessman to run the city and promising to boost local businesses. I asked my team to find out who had printed it, and it turned out it had been printed in Houston. At high noon I walked down the steps of city hall to the chairs. The media were all there. I checked my watch—twelve o'clock—and looked over at the empty seat. "Well, it appears that Mr. Monfrey is not accepting my challenge," I said. "I have brought along this little newspaper that he has published. Perhaps he wants us to read it instead of appearing in person."

I began reading an article on the front page in which Mr. Monfrey claimed that San Antonio businessmen were not supporting our city as well as they should be. Mr. Monfrey went on to say that he would bring business to San Antonio and not have it go to other places. "That sounds interesting," I continued, "but we've noticed this little newspaper he had produced was printed in Houston. Does that sound like a businessman who wants to bring business to San Antonio?" Soon after that, a joke started circulating that Mr. Monfrey didn't show up for the debate because he was sick—he had chickenpox.

I won the reelection, and that was the first year that our new districting system went into effect. The city council was expanded from nine members, including the mayor, to eleven. Ten members were elected from the districts they would represent, and the mayor was elected at large by the entire city.

Other members for the new term were Henry G. Cisneros, District 1; Joe Webb, District 2; Helen Dutmer, District 3; Frank D. Wing, District 4; Bernardo Eureste, District 5; Rudy C. Ortiz, District 6; Joe Alderete Jr., District 7; Phil Pyndus, District 8; Glen Hartman, District 9; and John Steen, District 10. With this change in the election procedure, city council changed too. Under the GGL model, council members were primarily businesspeople, inclined to work as a team, with less controversy in terms of issues. With the new system, the council became more independent and complex because there were many different interests represented.

~

We had entered the era of the federal Urban Development Action Grants, and we had much more money to fight over, about $16 million for the city. At the same time, we were working on a bond election. We finally got to the point where we agreed on the development package that the $16 million would fund. We also worked through the proposals for the bond election and agreed on the projects to present for a vote at the next council meeting. The city clerk wrote out the ordinance. Everything was exactly as the council had decided it would be. Then Bernardo

Eureste raised his hand and said, "Mayor, I have an amendment."

He pulled out his paper and proposed an amendment to the entire program, altering everything the council had agreed to in previous meetings. Many of our central city projects had been thrown out, and the council majority voted for Councilman Eureste's set of projects. Our negotiated package was no longer viable.

The next day I called a press conference for 10 a.m., well attended by the media. I announced what had happened in city council the day before. I explained that only a little over half of the members were informed of the new proposal. "Under these circumstances," I said, "I am going to ask the citizens of San Antonio to vote no on the upcoming bond issue."

It was unheard of for a mayor to tell the public to vote no on a bond issue, but I was committed to running a council that worked together in good faith and respected each member, as we are sworn to do. I told the press that the programs were not created in this spirit, and I asked the public to reject them. Of course, the media ran to the members who had changed the package, and they told the press they were confident that they would get the amended bond issue passed. I continued to say, "Citizens, this is the time to say no, until the council shows it is going to work together." The bond issue was defeated 60 percent to 40 percent, which was a rude awakening for the council. Although the members who wanted the amendments represented a majority on the council, they did not represent a majority of the city. That was a difficult time; everyone had some growing up to do.

One morning Councilman Eureste arrived at city hall in a bad mood. It seemed that nothing happening in the meeting was to his liking; he kept hopping out of his seat and interrupting. He was not behaving himself as a young man should, and he certainly showed no respect for the presiding officer, namely me. Finally I'd had enough. I looked over at Bernardo and said, very formally, "The gentleman will take his seat." He was standing, shaking his shoulders, unsmiling, and he did not respond. I repeated the request a second time and then a third time. "I don't have to do that!" he said.

I looked around and asked if there was a police officer in the room. The chief of police happened to be present. Without raising my voice, I asked him to escort Mr. Eureste from the chamber. Bernardo was so surprised that he did not know what to say or do.

He meekly walked out with the police chief, and we continued the meeting. In about fifteen minutes, a handwritten note from Bernardo was brought to me, asking if he could come back if he promised to stay in his seat. I sent word that he could return. He came back and quietly took his seat in a respectful way.

The next day Bernardo knocked on my office door and came in. "Mayor," he said, "I have been thinking about what happened yesterday when you had the officer escort me out of the room. I'm not sure you really had the authority to do that."

"Well, Bernardo," I said, "I'm not positive I did either. But you didn't think of that yesterday, did you?"

We both had a good laugh. I have always thought laughter is the cure for many things. We both got over that incident, and although Bernardo had what I would call a quick trigger—a tendency to rise to anger quickly—he learned to calm down and rethink his situation before lashing out. We really got along much better than it might have appeared on the surface.

As we were learning to work together, the council hired a new city manager in 1977. Thomas Huebner came from Sacramento, California, and he was a real

professional. Several of us on the council, including
Henry Cisneros, Glen Hartman, and myself, gave
him a mandate to appoint more women and minorities to his city administrative staff. Mr. Huebner
was very amenable to this because he wanted his
top city-appointed officials to reflect the diversity
of our city. There were still Anglo men appointed,
but they did not automatically get the jobs as they
had previously. He appointed two young Latinos as
his assistants, Alex Briseño and Rolando Bono; later
each would serve as city manager. He also appointed
Jane Macon as the city attorney. At age twenty-nine,
she was the youngest city attorney in the nation;
her brilliant work helped San Antonio's economic
development in major ways.

~

My radar was always acute when I learned that someone notable was going to be in our vicinity. I liked
to invite well-known people to visit San Antonio
so we could show them our wonderful city and let
our citizens get a firsthand look at these prominent
international figures. I learned that Prince Charles
was coming to Texas at the invitation of Anne Armstrong, who had served as the U.S. ambassador to

the Court of Saint James in London. The prince was planning to play polo at the Armstrong ranch, which was only a few hundred miles from San Antonio.

We contacted Prince Charles through the British consul in Houston, and he accepted our invitation to add San Antonio to his schedule. When we discussed proper international protocol with the consul general, I learned that strict rules would require the prince to ride from the airport in the first car with me, and that his chief of staff would ride in the second car with my husband. I thought about how much Sid would enjoy being in the first car with me and the prince, and I brought this up once more before the scheduled visit. Word came back that we needed to follow protocol, and of course we did.

When Prince Charles disembarked at the airport, I greeted him with Sid standing next to me. The prince stepped up to shake Sid's hand and said, "Sorry about the car, old chap, but even my dad has to ride in the second car sometimes." I was astonished that he had even heard about the protocol discussion, and we all chuckled together.

The Winston Churchill High School band welcomed the prince with a rousing concert at the airport, and four young drum majorettes were in front of the instrument section. In the interest of Anglo

When Prince Charles visited San Antonio, he was greeted like a rock star by citizens of all ages.

American relations, the prince decided to personally greet each of these young ladies. He shook hands down the row. When we got into the car to go to the hotel, he was seated to my right in the back seat. I looked over at him and noticed he had a funny expression on his face. I asked if everything was all right; he laughed and opened his hand. As he had gone down the line, one of the young ladies had put her picture in his hand. We turned it over, and there was her telephone number.

My second term seemed to speed by, filled with colorful characters, interesting issues, and important decisions. During my entire time in public office—on the city council and as mayor—there was always an issue relating to water. Sometimes I laughingly say that I never met a water plan I didn't love. San Antonio constantly repeated its cycle of extended droughts, when everyone would cry and grieve and come up with a new water plan, followed by lots of rain, when people would decide we did not need any more water plans. It is hard to get people's attention once it starts raining and the drought is over. Over many years I tried to support every plan that could possibly add to our water supply.

The Applewhite surface reservoir was one proposal, but it failed. I realized there were some legitimate questions about how much water would be lost through evaporation. On the other hand, I felt that any water we could capture would be valuable. There were water plans for building dams that would bring water from Cibolo and Cuero, but construction would be expensive and our city felt it did not have the budget for these. Another project almost passed, losing by just one vote on the council. It was a plan that involved partnering with the Guadalupe-Blanco River Authority to guarantee that San Antonio could take up to 50,000 acre-feet of water annually from their sources for $1 million a year. I kept pointing out that it would take us a hundred years, paying $1 million a year, to reach the $100 million that a new dam or reservoir would cost. It did not pass, however.

Protection of the Edwards Aquifer, where San Antonio gets its water, was also an important issue during the 1970s building boom, and it continues to be so today. When real estate developers began to come up with proposals for building over the Edwards Aquifer Recharge Zone, we realized we had not done sufficient research and did not have the information we needed to make decisions to best protect it. No one wanted to turn a blind eye and allow the aquifer to be polluted, and there was a definite need for careful research and consideration about how to best put regulations in place. Of course, this infringed on the ability of developers to move forward with projects that they were ready to build. All of this needed to be discussed by all sides, taking the time to work through all the aspects of the issue. This is part of what makes city government work; sometimes it is not exciting, but it is necessary.

I loved city government—all parts—so much that

I ran for a third mayoral term in 1979; my opponent was former mayor Charles Becker. Despite my dislike of political fundraising and my low campaign budget, I prevailed and was reelected.

~

One Sunday morning, early in my third term as mayor, Sid and I were having breakfast, happily enjoying our morning coffee, when the telephone rang. It was a UPI reporter, who asked for my reaction to the fact that the shah of Iran was reportedly in San Antonio. I nearly dropped the receiver (we had only landlines then) with surprise. I asked him for the facts he had. The reporter told me that the shah and his wife had arrived at Kelly Air Force Base at midnight and had traveled to Lackland Air Force Base, where they were staying in the officers' quarters because the shah would be undergoing cancer treatment at Wilford Hall hospital.

I admitted to the reporter that I was unaware of this situation, but given the political sensitivities of the time, I felt sure the president of the United States must have authorized the trip. I realized it could raise quite a reaction from the public but assured him that the citizens of San Antonio were law-abiding, good citizens and that our city could handle this surprise.

Dining with Shah Mohammad Reza Pahlavi and his wife,
Empress Farah Diba Pahlavi, in 1979 was a memorable
evening for Sid and me.

As soon as I hung up, I telephoned a woman from
Texas who was on the White House staff and asked
if she had forgotten to tell me something. She said,
"Oops!" I told her that when the shah of Iran, an
internationally known figure who elicited strong
political reactions, is coming to your city and will

be there a while, the mayor should be notified. I assured her we were going to do what we could do to smooth the situation, but I was worried that his presence could raise some concerns. And so it did.

First thing Monday morning I called Lackland and talked to the commanding general, offering him city support if it was needed. We wanted to be helpful but not intrusive. He thanked me, and the next day he invited Sid and me to attend a small dinner party for the shah and the empress. There would be only eight people at the dinner—Maj. Gen. William P. Acker and his wife, retired four-star general Bennie Davis and his wife, the shah and the empress, and Sid and me.

We were there for more than four hours, and it was one of the most fascinating evenings of my life. The shah and his wife wanted to talk and talk; I gathered that in Iran the shah had been surrounded by people who never let him out of the palace. According to him, in recent years he had not had much direct contact with the people of his country; he was totally bewildered by the unrest. The empress kept asking, "How could all of this have happened? He has been so good to the women of Iran. He did so much for them." They were wringing their hands in disbelief. I knew the shah was ill, but his illness was not apparent that night. What was most obvious was his surprise that his people were turning against him and that there was going to be a coup in Iran. He must have had a powerful protective group surrounding him, preventing the news from outside from reaching him inside the palace. Later the world would learn more about his SAVAK secret service and the horrors going on in Iran, and I would think about impressions we form before history instructs us otherwise.

His wife was a beautiful young woman, filled with pent-up energy. The military command knew she was a good tennis player, and they found officers to take her to the tennis courts at the base to help her expend some of that energy and frustration.

The day after the dinner party, the shah's nephew was assassinated in Paris. Lackland Air Force Base was immediately closed to outside visitors. Sid and I were grateful for that small window of time when we were able to meet the shah and his empress.

As I had anticipated, there were consequences to their presence in San Antonio. First, four young Iranian students attending San Antonio College protested at city hall. The city attorney, Jane Macon, and I worried about the attention the students were attracting. It escalated when radio personality Ricci

Ware announced, "If the mayor can't get them off of those steps, I'll go down and throw them off." Other radio and television announcers fueled public reaction, and we had to put the students in protective custody.

Meanwhile other Iranian students in town rallied and started a petition to have an anti-shah parade. They took the first step of applying for a permit with the police department. The police felt the parade would be a threat to public peace and declined the permit. Then the students appealed to the city manager. Tom Huebner came to my office to tell me that he was going to support the police chief in denying the parade permit. He warned me that the group might take the next step and appeal to the city council. They did.

By this time the incident started getting national media attention. The students made their appeal to city council, and we called a special meeting for them to be heard. I was never a dictatorial kind of mayor, telling people what they had to do, but this was one time I made an exception. I visited with everyone on the council and told them the plan.

"We don't want this to turn into a big national story," I said. "So we will have this hearing. It will be an open meeting where we will receive their request.

Then we are going to declare the hearing closed, and in closed session we are going to take a vote and we are going to vote 100 percent to support the city manager's decision to deny the permit." We had a special meeting called at night, and national media were there waiting for something big to happen. The council chamber was packed, and we let the students present their petition. We followed the scenario I had outlined, closing the meeting and unanimously voting to deny the petition for a permit. During all my years on the council, I loved a full debate, but this situation was just too volatile. There was no further discussion. It was handled, and we departed.

～

The opportunities for San Antonio to participate on the international stage were always important to me, and during all the terms I served as mayor, I had an amazing "right hand" named Shirl Thomas, who was a master at arranging the visits of foreign dignitaries. She had been an intern for Mayor Becker when she was a student at Trinity University, and I hired her as my administrative assistant in 1975. In addition to assisting with our international visitors, she worked with me on the U.S. Conference of Mayors and the National League of Cities, and she was an absolute treasure at city hall. Shirl worked in city government for eighteen years, assisting several of the mayors that came after me, and eventually worked in Washington as special assistant to Henry Cisneros when he served as secretary of housing and urban development.

I had watched Henry work hard as a city councilman for the past six years, and I admired his innovative spirit and good ideas for San Antonio. As 1981 approached and I contemplated running for a fourth term as mayor, something unexpected happened in my life. Now I contemplated big changes, and I began to think about Henry Cisneros in a new role.

TEN

Changes

Surprises in life happen; some are wonderful, and some are not. My beloved husband, Sid Cockrell, had been my constant source of love and support for nearly forty years, and when he began having serious heart problems during my third term as mayor, I wanted to give him my full support. He had been so patient during all the years I was in public life, so cooperative and encouraging every time I ran for and held a political office. It was my turn to reciprocate. I decided not to run for reelection in 1981.

I did not want to announce my decision too early, however, and become a lame duck. Henry Cisneros was waiting rather impatiently; he did not want to tread on my toes by announcing his candidacy if I was thinking about running again. I told him I would make a statement soon. First I told my special group of political supporters, which included many of the city's business leaders, that I would not seek another term.

At that time, if I did not run for reelection, the GGL had a choice of backing Henry or John Steen. John Steen was a fine man and community leader, a respected gentleman in every way. Henry was a young, energetic candidate. Both had qualities to make them excellent choices, and I think the GGL hierarchy had a difficult time deciding which one to back. One would be a more traditional type of mayor, an Anglo business leader like many we had had before; the other was Hispanic and highly innovative and would no doubt have a lot of new programs and ideas bursting forth. The GGL chose to back Henry, and I knew it was the right decision. John Steen was an exemplary man, but Henry could move the city forward in ways it never had moved before.

~

Henry served four terms as mayor. He was—and is—my good friend, and I felt strongly that it was not my place to hover over him with ideas or advice. He was a self-starter, a brilliant young man who was eager to chart exciting vistas for San Antonio. Of course, I told him I would be happy to help with

I believed that if Henry Cisneros was elected mayor in 1981, he would move San Antonio forward in exciting ways with his energy and big dreams for the city.

background on any issue if there was information he did not have; I was just a telephone call away.

Now that I was out of office, I thought Sid and I should do something fun together. We signed up for a Caribbean cruise that began in San Juan, Puerto Rico. When I was a member of the U.S. Conference of Mayors, I had become friends with San Juan's mayor, Carlos Romero Barceló, who was now the governor. I also knew his mayoral successor, Hernán

Padilla Ramirez, and I thought Sid and I could offer to host them both for dinner aboard our ship before we sailed. I put in a telephone call to each man's office to invite him.

A few days later I was accompanying Henry Cisneros to Austin for a meeting he'd asked me to attend, and I mentioned that I was hoping to see my two friends in Puerto Rico. I told him I had not heard back from either.

"Uh-oh," Henry said. "You must not know."

"Know what?" I asked. He told me that Hernán was running as a gubernatorial candidate against Carlos. "Ohhhhhhh," I said. "I did not know that."

A week or more went by. About two weeks before our departure, I had a call from Hernán declining the invitation because of a National Guard obligation. While I was sorry to miss him, his call was a great relief. I still had not heard from Carlos, although Sid had mentioned receiving a long-distance call that he had not been able to understand.

We arrived in Puerto Rico and boarded the ship at 5 p.m. I soon realized what that telephone call Sid had mentioned was about. A few minutes after we checked into our stateroom, the purser telephoned to say that the military aide to the governor of Puerto Rico was onboard, asking where the dinner for the governor was to take place. I told the aide that I was delighted to learn that the governor and his wife were coming, then quickly asked the purser to arrange for this exciting surprise. The ship laid on the dinner beautifully, and no one would have known it was planned only a few hours beforehand. The governor and his wife arrived, and we dined on shrimp cocktails and grilled steaks. The ship did not sail until midnight. Our guests were very happy—they had never visited a cruise ship before. And the cruise ship had never hosted a governor of Puerto Rico before; the staff was excited to do so. It all turned out fine, much to my relief!

Because Sid and I loved to travel, when Chip Atkins offered me the presidency of his travel agency, I was tempted to accept the opportunity to work in the private sector. But although I had given a tentative yes, three of San Antonio's top business leaders asked me to lead an organization they had dreamed up to boost the city's economic development. Gen. Robert F. McDermott, Tom Frost, and B.J. "Red" McCombs felt that the promotion of economic growth in the city was being compromised; one prospect had recently been lost due to local wrangling. They asked me to accept an appointment as executive director of a new organization, United

San Antonio. My love for San Antonio compelled me to accept, and I made my apologies to Chip with a promise to work for him in the future.

~

At United San Antonio we looked at a range of city issues, including the high illiteracy rate, inequalities related to property values in our many school districts, and the need for college engineering courses at the University of Texas at San Antonio (UTSA), which had been established a little more than a decade before. Getting approval from the University of Texas Board of Regents and the University System Coordinating Board for those courses was not easy, but we prevailed. Henry Cisneros made the final pitch during our presentation in Austin; he was spectacular, and we got almost unanimous approval, with just one vote against us.

The three years I worked with United San Antonio were satisfying. I felt like I had done something constructive, helped create a bridge to the future. When my commitment there was over, I got to realize my dream to run a travel agency. It was a much easier business to run than that of a city, and I enjoyed it. Sid and I took some great trips together and treasured those precious years through 1985.

Travel adventures with Sid in the early 1980s
spanned the globe.

My tall, handsome Sid was a wonderful husband, one of the most honorable persons one could ever know. He protected his family, and I always knew he would do the right thing. He never felt the least bit threatened by my public life. I think that takes a man who is comfortable within his identity. Sid had his own leadership roles in the community, and we had a blessed marriage. He loved our daughters. Some people who go into public life don't have happy marriages, but we had a wonderful one. In February 1986 Sid passed away of congestive heart failure. That was a very hard time for me. There was never anyone else in my life, never of Sid's quality. After his death I finally started to go out with some gentlemen friends, intelligent, accomplished, thoughtful widowers, including Al Eckhardt, a good friend of Sid's; Bill Ochse, a businessman and owner of the Saint Anthony Hotel; businessman Walter Corrigan; Norman "Pinky" Hill, former general manager of the San Antonio Transit Company; Jack Spruce, general manager of CPS Energy; Brig. Gen. Robert F. McDermott, president of USAA; businessman Tom Berg, CPS Energy board chair; and Brig. Gen. Julius Braun, all now deceased. I was appreciative of their friendship, but I never met another Sid and I have never been tempted to marry again. I traveled

I traveled with friends Jane Macon (*left*) and Patricia Smothers
(*right*) when the International Women's Forum honored
Prime Minister Margaret Thatcher.

as a widow with my mother, daughters, or friends
and continued to run the travel agency for a while.
But I began to want to do something new.

I had remained close to Henry Cisneros, and in fall
1988, after some media speculation, he announced
that he would not run for reelection. I had been
visiting with him in his office before he spoke to the
media, and when I left, members of the press were

hanging around, asking me if I might run again. As I recall, I responded that if Henry was sure he would not run, I would give it some thought.

I had been surprised by Henry's announcement. I began contacting some of the business leaders who had been my backers in earlier campaigns and who went on to support Henry when I did not run in 1981. There were some mixed signals from Henry's political supporters over the next few months, but by now most of his major financial supporters had committed to my candidacy. There were also rumors that Councilman Nelson Wolff might run. But neither Henry nor Nelson did, and I was elected mayor again in 1989.

It proved to be a difficult term. A number of bond issues had passed while Henry was mayor, and San Antonio went into a recession, like many other cities at the time. San Antonio Savings Association went under with serious defaults; many other banks and savings and loans were also having a difficult time. I had inherited most of Henry's city council, and my style was different from his. Henry was more of a strong leader type, always out in front, setting the pace. I was more of the consensus-building type. It took the council a little time to get used to me, and I worked hard getting used to them.

Lou Fox had been appointed city manager when Henry was mayor, and the two had an excellent relationship. But a new police contract under consideration had become very controversial. Lou Fox, based on his staff's reports, had announced that the contract, which included additional compensation, would have a $17 million impact on the city budget over the next five years, if accepted. That estimate, however, turned out to be not fully accurate. From the first year to the last, with the compounding effect, it would actually amount to more than $50 million. The city council had agreed to approve the contract; then news broke about the reported discrepancy. The error was blamed on the city manager. The increases for each year had been added together to come up with the $17 million figure, and the council had voted based on that information, not the total compounded impact. The media covered the story in a big way, and Lou was blamed for reporting incorrect information to the council. The issue put a damper on Henry's last few months as mayor and created distrust among the city staff and within the community. That was the overall mood when I returned to office.

With the city still unhappy about the police contract, there was a second one to deal with. The police contract had come first but had not received the final vote. Now the firefighters contract was before the council. It had gone through the vetting process and been approved in the council's B Session, but it had not been voted on. I felt that since the police contract had been approved informally by the prior council and just required a final vote, I should honor that commitment, and I took the same position on the firefighters contract. It was controversial among the citizens of San Antonio, but I voted with the council, feeling that we could not approve one contract and not the other. The contracts would ensure stability within the ranks of our police and fire defenders, and while I did not set up the situation, I dealt with it as best I could. Many people were unhappy with us.

Without question, I felt the city manager or his staff had made a mistake, but I knew that overall Lou Fox had built a fine, distinguished career. I knew he had not underestimated the police contract deliberately, though the media was calling for his termination. He resigned a few months later and became the city manager of Lubbock, Texas.

Alex Briseño became San Antonio's new city manager, and we worked very well together. He ran a straight, sharp office. I admired him very much; he was one of the best parts of my fourth term as mayor.

Alex went on to be one of our most outstanding and long-serving city managers.

Another highlight was a visit from a second president of Mexico. In 1991 President Carlos Salinas and about half of his cabinet came to the city as official guests and to tour the Splendors of Mexico exhibit at the San Antonio Museum of Art. We were pleased and honored to show the exhibit in our city, one of only three venues in the United States. The other two were New York's Metropolitan Museum of Art and the Los Angeles County Museum of Art.

President Salinas was easy to host and was pleased with the extraordinary exhibit. Unlike President Echeverría, who danced to his own tune in a wonderfully unpredictable way, President Salinas was more traditional. During the visit, there was an unhappy surprise, but it was not his fault.

As a matter of courtesy, I had extended an invitation to Texas governor Ann Richards to be an official guest at the exhibit opening, thinking a member of her staff would drive her to San Antonio. Instead, upon learning of President Salinas's participation, she contacted his office to insist that he come to Austin first to be officially received by her, as governor, and the Texas Legislature. She also advised him that she would be happy to join him on his plane for a continuing trip to San Antonio.

When my staff heard about this, my executive assistant, Shirl Thomas, added a second official car to meet the plane at the airport, and I asked mayor pro tem Nelson Wolff and his wife, Tracy, to join me in serving as official hosts and ride in the second car with the governor.

When President Salinas's plane arrived and he and Governor Richards disembarked, however, she stayed right with President Salinas and me as we walked to the first car. She pushed her way into the middle of the back seat between the president and me. My staff was dismayed at the break in protocol, and so was I.

$\sim$

We went directly to the museum, where the president of the Museum Association and her board were waiting in a receiving line to greet the president. The museum board had raised a huge amount of money for the Splendors of Mexico exhibit, and I planned to present President Salinas, then step aside to allow Alice Reynolds, the museum's president, to host him as he toured the exhibit. As we approached the receiving line, Governor Richards again grabbed President Salinas by the arm, rushed past the board

Queen Elizabeth and Prince Philip's visit to San Antonio was a highlight for me in 1990.

members, and entered the exhibit. The museum board and I were trotting along behind them, and the museum people felt that their hard work to put on this wonderful event had been ignored. I was so disappointed in Governor Richards's behavior because, as a woman, I wanted to be supportive of our female governor. I had never seen her do anything like that.

My staff was furious, and for me it was a sad day for the "sisterhood."

A much happier experience with a state visit occurred toward the end of my term. Queen Elizabeth and Prince Philip of England came to San Antonio during the queen's tour of the United States. We worked hard to get on her itinerary. The city had hosted Prince Charles more than a decade before, and there was much excitement when we learned his royal parents would be our guests.

I took the royal couple on a river barge tour, of course, which is always included as a highlight for anyone visiting San Antonio—it's true for presidents, sports stars, movie stars, royalty, and people like you and me. Like everyone I've ever taken on a river cruise, they were enchanted. Next we visited the Institute of Texan Cultures, with exhibits that represent all of the countries that have influenced our multicultural state. The British exhibit was of special interest, of course, and special invited guests joined our entourage for a lovely lunch in honor of the royal couple. My dear friend Rosemary Kowalski, whose catering company had grown to quite an empire since those early HemisFair days, was in charge of the meal, and it was spectacular. Today she laughingly remembers that special day when we were "both at the queen's elbows"—I was sitting next to Her Majesty, and Rosemary was presenting her with a gin and tonic.

In addition to visiting San Antonio, Queen Elizabeth went to three other Texas cities—Dallas, Austin, and Houston. She concluded her tour by hosting a beautiful dinner at the Houston Museum of Fine Arts and invited mayors of the cities she had visited and their special guests. I asked General McDermott to be my escort. He was a widower, not yet remarried, and was very pleased to go. We flew to Houston in the USAA plane, along with city manager Alex Briseño and his wife, who were also invited to the dinner. The evening was special—I was seated at table number two, between Prince Philip and the famous heart surgeon Dr. Michael DeBakey. Unfortunately General McDermott was seated at a different table, reminding me of those many years ago when Prince Charles visited San Antonio and Sid had to ride in the second car.

∼

Glamorous evenings were just a small part of my mayoral duties. I spent most days and evenings on more serious matters, like approving the city's annual budget. The city council and I had developed a good

working relationship, and we were determined
to adopt a realistic budget for 1990. C.A. Stubbs's
Homeowner-Taxpayer Association was very active
in San Antonio, constantly complaining about costs
and tax rates, and it was promoting a much more
conservative budget for the new fiscal year. After lots
of discussion at council meetings, I supported the
realistic budget, and the association started a petition
calling for a referendum. If I had pulled back and
supported the really "bare bones" budget, and not
supported the majority of the council, I could have
avoided the referendum. But I decided to support
that majority, and it was an unpopular stand with
San Antonio's voters. I knew the position was risky. I
realized I could have helped my own political standing by renouncing the council's wishes, but that did
not feel right. We approved the more realistic budget, and that stance proved costly in the upcoming
mayoral race.

During my last campaign there were eleven candidates for mayor, including four council members—
Nelson Wolff, Maria Berriozábal, and ultraconser-
vatives Jimmie Hasslocher and Van Archer. I ended
up in third place, with Nelson Wolff and Maria
Berriozábal in the runoff election. I was contacted
later by many shocked voters who told me they had

planned to vote for me in the "final" election and had voted in the primary for the other candidate they hoped would be my opponent in the runoff.

Maria was an ardent spokesperson for the poor and disadvantaged. She carried in her heart a deep passion for improving the lives of disadvantaged Hispanics, and I admired her for that. I thought she was so wrapped up in that one cause, however, that she would be perceived as a candidate who could not represent the entire city. Henry Cisneros, on the other hand, had worked closely with Hispanic, Anglo, and African American constituents, considered diverse agendas, and served all citizens. It could be done, and our city needed someone who could unify it.

Nelson Wolff defeated Maria Berriozábal in the runoff and was elected mayor in 1991. I had known Nelson for many years, from his career as a state senator and his years on the city council. I thought he was very bright, and he supported many of the causes that I thought were important.

I admired his many attempts to get a new state constitution, and I find it extraordinary that we still have not done that. We have a very old constitution that has been amended, and amended, and amended—so many times that it is often hard to figure it out. I still believe we need a new one.

Besides the good causes Nelson promoted in the state senate, his work on the city council was thoughtful and solid. He always had interesting ideas and perspectives, and I have always admired and liked him. His wife, Tracy, is also very gracious and talented, and both have been important contributors to our city.

~

The only election I ever lost was in 1991. I realized that people wanted a change. While I was disappointed to lose, I knew Nelson was a good, honorable person and would work hard as mayor. Some people feel depleted when they lose a political race; I did not. I had done what I thought was best, so the defeat never really fazed me. I congratulated Nelson, thanked San Antonio for the opportunity to serve, and moved on. I knew there were many other ways to serve the city I loved, and I would find them.

Looking back over the years I was on the council and the four terms I served as mayor, I realize that I worked with several city managers. In the council-manager form of government, which San Antonio has, the city manager position is similar to that of a corporate CEO. It's tremendously important.

The first manager I worked with was Jack Shelley,

Good friends and former mayors of San Antonio Henry
Cisneros (*left*) and Nelson Wolff (*right*) went on to serve as
U.S. secretary of HUD and Bexar County judge, respectively.
All three of us love our city, our county, and our country.

and I thought he was a very good, competent city
manager. When I joined the council, he realized he
would need to get used to my insistence on improving the number of board appointments for women
and other minorities. He had not thought it was all

that important in the beginning, but I'm happy to say he changed his mind.

Jerry Henckel was also a competent city manager, but I was aware of some personal issues that he had that were beginning to be talked about. He was followed by Loyd Hunt, who worked closely with Mayor Charles Becker. He was only in the position for about nine months.

Sam Granata Jr. had been a competent public works director whom I had always liked; he was named city manager when Mayor Becker was still in office. After I became mayor in 1975, he continued to meet with the former mayor, to report on what was going on at city hall. I was concerned, and other council members also became concerned, and his services were terminated. His assistant, Tom Raffety, served for a month or so while we searched for a new manager.

We found Tom Huebner, who was highly professional and a very fine city manager. He came to San Antonio after serving as city manager in Sacramento, California, and was active in the national city managers' association. For some in our community, his attire was a little too casual. Tom wore a lot of guayaberas, which he thought were appropriate in San Antonio. Many felt he should wear the more formal coat and tie previous city managers had traditionally worn, and there was some criticism about that.

Dress codes aside, Tom was intelligent and effective, and he had to try to learn how to deal with some of our more flamboyant council members, like Bernardo Eureste. I remember receiving a telephone call as I was getting ready to leave for a National League of Cities meeting in Seattle, alerting me that Tom and Bernardo were having a feud. I called them into my office and told them I was aware of their disagreement and that I wanted them to declare a truce while I was out of town. Finally they both sheepishly agreed to shake hands.

In the car on the way to the airport, I got a call from Tom. He said, "Mayor, I don't think I can live up to the truce agreement." I was stern and told him they had to behave themselves while I was gone. They did, kind of. Both were strong-minded men, and they never got along well. I think I became kind of a mother figure to most of the council members I worked with, and I often used humor to deflect a difficult situation, especially with Bernardo. I would tease him slightly, urging him to behave like a good boy. Henry Cisneros and Glen Hartman, who had a brilliant mind, were some of the easiest council members to work with, and both were totally supportive of my directives to Tom to look for additional qualified women and minorities to fill prominent city staff positions.

Tom appointed his two assistant city managers, Alex Briseño and Rolando Bono. Both were graduates of Trinity University and had earned advanced degrees in urban studies. They both later became city managers. Alex was our longest-term city manager until Sheryl Sculley was hired several decades later.

One of the best things Tom did was to appoint Jane Macon city attorney. She was a wiz, and she and Tom instigated some important economic development successes for the city, including the Rivercenter Mall project. They used new urban development funding programs like Urban Development Action Grants and built public-private partnerships that encouraged the development of the downtown area.

Of course, as a city develops, all sorts of citizen groups form, and members of those were frequent visitors to council meetings. I found it was interesting to hear from our citizens. The groups were diverse, ranging from COPS to the San Antonio Conservation Society and the Chamber of Commerce. When rate hikes were contemplated for our water and utility services, representatives from those boards would appear to ask the council to approve the increases. And there always were what I called the regular visitors, who liked to speak every week in the special "citizens to be heard" portion of the meeting, letting us know everything we were doing wrong.

I've always known it is impossible to please everyone. Early on I established my guiding principles, influenced profoundly by my strong grandmother and my deep respect for all the voices in a room—or a city. As I left the mayor's office in 1991, I knew I would find new ways to listen to San Antonio's dreams and that I would continue to work hard to make them come true.

ELEVEN

San Antonio, I Love You

1991–2018

Not long after I had left the mayor's office, the city asked me to assemble a group to travel to Kumamoto for a festival celebrating the anniversary of our Sister Cities relationship. We were expected to bring a band along with the delegation, and we selected Little Joe y La Familia, a wonderful Tejano group that had seven musicians. The contract was signed, but about three days before the trip, the band leader called me to say we had a big problem. One of his musicians was quite ill and could not make the journey. The contract was precise and called for a seven-person band. I asked Little Joe if he knew anybody who could take the musician's place, and he said he had called everybody he could think of and nobody could go. They either had other commitments or did not have travel documents.

The next day I shared my worries with my

daughter Carol, as I was not sure what we would do with the trip just two days away. She reminded me that she was a musician and had a passport, and she said she would like to go. I quickly called Little Joe with the good news, and I'm sure he thought, Uh-oh! He had never heard Carol play and had no idea how she would fit in with the group. But when we arrived in Japan and they rehearsed together, Little Joe was thrilled. "This girl is good," he said. "We need to hire her!" The band, with Carol on the accordion, was a big hit in Kumamoto, and the trip was a great success.

~

After we returned, tragedy struck our family. My brother Andrew called me at the travel agency to tell me that my mother and other brother, Ovid, had been murdered. I was devastated and could hardly process the news.

My mother had inherited the apartment house my grandmother had owned and operated. Both of my brothers were tenants, and my mother lived there as well. Mother, who was ninety years old, lived in the largest apartment, which had been my grandmother's home. Ovid shared that apartment since he was not married and helped Mother in her senior years. My brother Andrew lived in another building in the same complex. He received the call that something was wrong, went to their apartment, and found my mother and Ovid murdered.

The crime was thought to have occurred around midnight or 1 a.m. My brother was found in the living room still holding the book he had been reading. It appeared that Mother had heard a disturbance and was walking into the room from her bedroom. The police made a thorough investigation but were never able to come up with clues. They surmised that the murderer had broken in, looking for valuables. It was reported that a person had been seen prowling around the complex around midnight. But no evidence was ever found linking an individual to the crime, and it was never solved.

Although my mother was ninety, hers was an untimely death. She enjoyed traveling and was very active, and she had many, many friends. My brother was only sixty-three. The tragedy of it all has continued to haunt me.

Memories of Mother came flooding back for months, of course, and when the new San Antonio Museum of Art asked me to join their board, I thought about the special excursions I took with Mother to the Metropolitan Museum, the Cloisters

Museum, and the Museum of Modern Art when we lived in New York. From those first glimpses of great paintings when I was a child, I had developed an appreciation for art, and I was happy to accept the invitation to join the museum's board. After years as one organization, the San Antonio Museum Association was splitting into two separate museums—the Witte Museum, which housed mostly natural history exhibits, and the San Antonio Museum of Art. My friend Lenora Brown was the art museum's organizing chairperson. In the first organizational discussions, we set an early goal to establish a wing for Latin American art, which, of course, would require raising some big money.

Soon after, I read in the newspaper that the city council was holding a hearing on the next bond issue that very day. I telephoned Lenora immediately, told her about the bond election coming up, and asked if she had discussed the funding for the new wing with the mayor. She told me she had mentioned it to Nelson a few years earlier. I told her we needed to get to the hearing that afternoon and that we needed to get our troops there too.

The museum staff called all of the board members, asking them to come to the meeting and to bring other art aficionados with them. Lenora asked if I would make the pitch to the council, and I did. They listened politely.

Usually a bond program is well set by the time there is a public hearing, and the council had a proposed plan when I made my pitch. I stressed that the funds would be for a Latin American center and what it would do for San Antonio's economic development. The bond vote was scheduled for the next week. A few days later I happened to run into Nelson, who told me he had good news—the council had found some money for the museum. I thanked him and asked how much. "Half a million," he responded.

"Oh, Nelson, that won't do," I said. "We have to have a million. I know you can do that, Nelson. I'm counting on it."

The day it was presented at city council, the bond issue vote was scheduled for three o'clock in the afternoon. Nelson announced the vote would be postponed an hour because they were still working on some of the numbers. At 4 p.m. the bond was rolled out, and the Museum of Art was included, with $1 million for the Latin American center.

At eight o'clock the next morning my telephone rang. It was Nelson, and of course I thanked him profusely. He told me that the council had been discussing who should be the chairperson for the bond election, and that I had been unanimously selected. I knew it was payback time.

I knew that to do the job well, I would need to work hard. I stepped away from my board duties at the museum and began to focus. In those days it was customary to raise at least $200,000 for the promotion of a bond issue, to cover advertising and other publicity to get it passed. The financial committee told me they thought it would take at least that amount, but I thought we could do it for less.

The dollars for promotion must come from the private sector, and since corporations and individuals benefit from the proposals, they are expected to participate financially. I was always frugal when it came to spending dollars contributed by the public, and I suggested that we get the neighborhood associations that had money coming to their communities from the bond election to organize citizen participation and support. The finance committee had raised $100,000 when I told them to stop their fundraising for promotion. The 1994 bond issue passed, and this is probably the only bond election in San Antonio's history where every contributor got back a third of his or her donation.

Once the bond election was nearing completion, the museum asked me to become its development director. Douglas Highland, the museum's new director, was a brilliant man from the New England art world. I liked him very much, but he had some challenges in San Antonio. He and the board often had different aesthetic tastes and intellectual interests—his eastern approach to art and social customs sometimes clashed with the southwestern style he encountered here. In what was a bold idea at the time, Dr. Highland suggested that the museum hold a special exhibition of the work of Jesse Treviño, a local Mexican American artist who had lost an arm in the Vietnam War and had become an extraordinary painter. Lenora and I were pushing for the exhibit, and the board rather grudgingly agreed to move forward. Attendance at the public opening was higher than for any prior museum exhibition or event—ever.

Dr. Highland also realized that one of our board members, Harriet Kelley, and her husband, Dr. Harmon Kelley, had one of the country's largest and most important collections of African American art. He worked with them to organize a wonderful exhibition of their paintings at the museum, followed by a national traveling exhibit that ended up at the Smithsonian. This was an important moment for San Antonio. I traveled to Washington to support the exhibit, so proud that our museum had created something so extraordinary that it made it to our nation's capital. Harriet and Harmon became close friends of mine, and many of the artworks in my own collection are by African American artists I discovered through them.

The Kelleys invited me to a reception they were hosting for a nationally known artist in their home. Their beautiful house was the perfect space to display their art collection, and I was mesmerized by what I saw. On the first floor they had works by internationally renowned artists I could recognize—serious art, art that I could never afford. When I reached the third floor, I saw that their informal sitting area was filled with works by local African American artists. Those paintings spoke to me. I was very touched by them, and I told Harriet that I loved what I had seen. She mentioned that one of the artists, John Coleman, was a guest at the reception and introduced me to him. The first painting I bought from him was of a jazz musician. Then I bought a second painting, *The Trumpet Player*, and I ended up buying several more from him.

As my interest in art deepened, I bought more paintings, some during the annual San Antonio Ethnic Arts exhibition, and others from artists

Thanks to art patrons Harriet Kelley and Aaronetta Pierce, I began to build my own collection of paintings by African American artist John Coleman in the 1990s.

that another great friend and art patron, Aaronetta Pierce, introduced me to. With time, I had an interesting collection of mostly African American artists; many paintings still hang in my home. A few years ago Port San Antonio mounted an exhibition of my entire collection, and since then I have started giving some of the paintings to Saint Philip's College each year.

My work at the San Antonio Museum of Art opened an exciting world to me, and I made some wonderful lifelong friends. But disagreements between the board and Douglas Highland escalated, and I decided to look for something else to do.

Beauty—whether found in paintings or nature—has always inspired me. When I left the museum, I found another way to pursue it. In 1997 I became the executive director of the San Antonio Parks Foundation. In a way it was like coming full circle—I had worked hard on preserving and improving our city's parks while I was on the council and during my terms as mayor, and I could do that again as a private citizen in the nonprofit sector.

~

While we completed many, many projects in parks all over town—from swimming pools to performing stages and special amenities—the largest project I directed was the restoration of the Japanese Tea Garden at Brackenridge Park. The garden dates back to 1917, when Ray Lambert, a parks commissioner, began developing lush gardens in an old rock quarry. Kimi Eizo Jingu, a local Japanese American artist, moved to the gardens in 1926 and opened a tea room. He and his family lived on the premises until 1942, when anti-Japanese sentiment resulted in their eviction. The facility was renamed the Chinese Sunken Gardens, and a Chinese American family took over operations until the early 1960s. I always had a soft spot for the gardens, remembering my mother's stories about walking there with my father when I was an infant.

I also remembered that when Carol was growing up, she took accordion lessons from a musician named Tony Rozance, who had a four-piece combo that sometimes played on Sunday afternoons in the garden gazebo. Carol was one of his best students and was invited to join him; her memories of the gardens were very special. Later, when Carol was teaching in Houston, her school took a spring break excursion to San Antonio. She insisted that the group see the Japanese Tea Garden, and she was so disappointed when she saw that it had fallen into terrible disrepair. She was one of the most interested spectators and ardent supporters when I got involved in its restoration.

Bonnie Conner was on the San Antonio Parks Foundation's board of directors. She was a former city council member and had always been interested in open spaces and parks. I approached her about organizing an auxiliary group called Friends of the

Parks; she agreed to do it and became its president. The friends group made the restoration of the Japanese Tea Garden their main cause and, along with the foundation, helped raise hundreds of thousands of dollars for the project.

I divided the garden restoration into four projects. The first phase was the development of the master plan, which would be expensive. We hired a well-known Houston firm, the SWA Group, to create the project's landscape plan, and San Antonio–based Alamo Architects as the project architects. After we went through the process of getting the master plan approved by the city council, the project became a public-private partnership. The city would contribute some of its bond issue funds toward it, and the foundation would raise substantial private donations. Alamo Architects developed early drawings to help attract donors and eventually created the final design for the project.

Our first design and construction project involved stabilizing the ponds and the waterfall, which would cost more than $1 million. I started writing grants. The Parks Foundation had received numerous small grants, but we needed big money for this project. I was able to get five granting organizations to give us $100,000 each. That $500,000 was a big chunk, and

The Japanese Tea Garden project was dear to my heart. My parents had picnics there in 1920. Nearly a hundred years later it was restored to become an exquisite jewel in San Antonio.

the rest of the money came from smaller grants and individual donations.

The gardens, with beautiful water features and landscaping, reopened to the public in 2008 with great fanfare that included a serenade of Japanese songs by Tafolla Middle School Japanese students accompanied on the keyboard by my daughter Carol, calligraphy and origami demonstrations, and an enormous cake shaped like the beautiful koi that swam in the ponds.

Members of the Jingu family attended, along with many local officials and the media.

But this was just the beginning; there was more to do to complete the massive renovation of this historic San Antonio treasure. Each phase of the restoration—the master plan, the grounds and gardens, the lighting, and finally the Jingu House itself—required a new fundraising campaign. According to the predictions of the master plan, I had raised all the money needed to complete restoration of the historic house, nearly $1 million. But when construction started, we learned there was virtually no foundation under the house. I do not know what kept it from sliding off its hill a long time ago. The foundation had to be retrofitted, which would cost another $100,000. We worked together to find a few places where we could cut costs, and the construction continued. Finally, in 2015, after nearly a decade of work, the Jingu House was completed. At the opening celebration, citizens of San Antonio enjoyed refreshments at the tea house and a jazz concert in the limestone amphitheater, surrounded by new lighted paths in the lower gardens, koi-filled ponds, and of course, the sixty-foot waterfall.

∼

While I was working at the Parks Foundation, I had the opportunity to interact again with the river I loved and to solve a problem it faced every day. It took three men on a barge, working many hours, to clean the river, and this occurred seven days a week. The process was long, and it was unattractive to watch. They had garbage pails on the barge, and they pulled out all sorts of terrible-looking trash and debris. It really was an awful sight on our gorgeous river. We learned that a vehicle existed that could clean rivers. It floated down the waterway and spread winglike nets that caught the debris. It cost $100,000. I raised that money for the Parks Foundation, and we signed a purchase order for the river sweeper. Because this was a prototype, we did not get the vehicle right away; then the company producing it got into financial trouble. Its former partners filed a lawsuit, and it looked like we were never going to get our vehicle. Since we had a contract to purchase the river sweeper and the former partners were holding it up, I suggested that we sue the former partners for denying our contract rights. The minute we filed that suit, things changed; we got our river sweeper, and it all worked out well.

In the meantime a huge, exciting plan for the

San Antonio River was gaining momentum. Ideas to enhance sections of the river that reached beyond its two-mile, beautifully developed downtown River Walk had been discussed for decades, and civic leaders like David Straus and Arthur "Hap" Veltman had made some good early progress. Finally, in 1998, a partnership of the City of San Antonio, Bexar County, the San Antonio River Authority, and the U.S. Army Corps of Engineers began to move forward with an ambitious public works project estimated at a cost of nearly $385 million.

The plan called for the U.S. Army Corps of Engineers to restore the section of the river that was south of downtown, which had been "straightened" into a concrete spillway by the Corps in the 1950s, as a way of diverting flood waters. Everyone recognized that it was not attractive and that the city's South Side deserved better. The San Antonio River Improvements Project would re-create the river's natural meandering course, restore habitat, and provide new parks and recreation areas. This portion of the project was named the Mission Reach because its seven miles of walking paths and bicycle trails would feature portals that led to the historic Spanish missions near the river. To the north of downtown, the Museum

Reach would become a four-mile urban park with landscaped sidewalks and public art and access to several museums in the area.

As early planning got under way, Mayor Howard Peak and Bexar County judge Cyndi Taylor Krier established the San Antonio River Oversight Commission to create an open forum for citizen input. My deep love for the river was well known, and I was appointed cochair of the commission. Architect Irby Hightower was the other cochair, and twenty-two civic leaders who represented diverse neighborhoods were appointed to serve with us. We met monthly for nearly a decade to oversee the planning, design, project management, construction, and funding of the largest public works project San Antonio has ever undertaken. A few years into the project, in 2003, the San Antonio River Authority created the San Antonio River Foundation to raise funds from the private sector for the amenities, including art, sidewalks, and beautiful landscaping, that would be needed. Now there were five partner organizations, and each presented regularly to the River Oversight Commission. Irby's background in urban design and passion for the river made him the ideal cochair. I loved working with him, and we are both proud of the development that has occurred so far. There is more to come for the river segments that stretch to the north and south of downtown.

In 2006, however, the fundraising partners had not yet hit their goals, and there were rumors that an important aspect of the Museum Reach might be eliminated because of its cost. The plan called for some expensive locks just north of downtown, to allow our colorful river barges to travel north past the San Antonio Museum of Art to a turning basin that would be built at the river level of the exciting new multiuse development project on the site of the old Pearl Brewery. When I heard a rumor that Mayor Phil Hardberger was considering removing the locks from the construction plan because of the high cost, I went to see him in his office. Before I left his office I got his promise that he would not take away the lock funding. Not long after that, Phil and the chairman of the San Antonio River Foundation, Edward "Sonny" Collins, convinced Ed Whitacre, the CEO of AT&T, to donate $5 million to the Museum Reach. The locks were saved—and named for AT&T.

When the Museum Reach was dedicated in 2009 and the first barge floated through the new locks, Phil invited me to join him at the opening ceremony. I was so happy when we sailed together upriver and

The San Antonio River Improvements Project achieved a major milestone in 2009 when the first barges sailed upriver through a specially designed lock system. Mayor Phil Hardberger and I were passengers on the maiden voyage.

he turned to me and said, "You were right, Lila. We needed these locks." I smiled in the sunshine of that moment, remembering a day many years before when I first fell in love with the San Antonio River and the city through which it flows.

A year or so later, the theater that carries my name, with its incredible mural facade created by Mexican artist Juan O'Gorman for HemisFair in 1968, got a total renovation. The special meeting room at river level that I fought so hard to keep in the original construction plans is in constant use. In fact, it was the site for both my eightieth and ninetieth birthday parties, which were, of course, arranged by the extraordinary Rosemary Kowalski, who recently celebrated her ninety-sixth birthday.

I am very appreciative to the voters of San Antonio for the five terms I served on the city council and the four terms I served as mayor, and I am so proud of all that our city has accomplished over the years. It has been very gratifying to see that progress documented in numerous historical archives; I think every public servant appreciates being recognized for playing a part in progress.

As someone who believes strongly that education is essential to our world's future, I treasure the four honorary degrees I've received: an Honorary Associate of Arts award from Alamo Community Colleges; an Honorary Doctor of Science from Our Lady of the Lake University; an Honorary Doctor of Humane Letters from my alma mater, Southern Methodist University; and an Honorary Doctor of Law from Saint Mary's University.

I enjoy thinking about all the international guests that San Antonio has hosted, and I remain

St. Mary's University
Resolution
Presented with Gratitude to

Lila Cockrell

Honorary Doctor of Laws

Whereas, Lila Cockrell, legendary public servant and former four-term Mayor of San Antonio, has spent many decades working to improve the City of San Antonio and the lives of its denizens;

Whereas, Lila Cockrell served 10 years on the San Antonio City Council before being elected in 1975 as the City's first female mayor, an office she held until 1981 and again from 1989 to 1991, making her the first woman elected to lead a major metropolis in the modern era;

Whereas, her public service began when she volunteered to serve in the WAVES branch of the United States Navy during World War II and continued during the 1950s when she served as President of the Dallas and San Antonio chapters of the League of Women Voters;

Whereas, Lila Cockrell has engaged in significant humanitarian pursuits including environmental protection and advocacy for civil rights for women and historically unrepresented ethnic minorities in San Antonio;

Whereas, while not a graduate of St. Mary's, her life and accomplishments bear witness to the University's mission as a Catholic and Marianist institution in so far as her policies as Mayor made civic representation by citizens of the West Side of San Antonio feasible;

Whereas, further, Mayor Lila Cockrell made access to funding and civic services for women and children more economical, the water system of San Antonio more sustainable, and the politics of the City and the state more open to the participation of women and representatives of previously excluded groups;

Whereas, after retiring from politics Lila Cockrell continued to serve her beloved city as President of the San Antonio Parks Foundation from 1998 until 2013 and has attended countless events over the years, meeting visitors to San Antonio from across the nation and around the world with grace and style;

Whereas, Lila Cockrell is a role model for women in government, a San Antonio icon, and a true pioneer in developing the City into one of the country's finest and most popular destinations for business and leisure while remaining true to its culture and traditions, and its importance as a historical treasure;

Whereas, Lila Cockrell's contributions reflect a long-lived dedication to service to the common good of the City of San Antonio, its communities, and the nation;

Now Therefore Let It Be Resolved, the administration, faculty and Board of Trustees of St. Mary's University recognize Lila Cockrell for her extraordinary leadership and outstanding service to the City of San Antonio; her influential impact on San Antonio politics; and for tirelessly and successfully serving our community for more than six decades with intelligence, sincerity and good humor and good will by presenting her with a Doctor of Laws, honoris causa, on this thirteenth day of May, in the year two thousand and seventeen.

Thomas M. Mengler

Thomas M. Mengler, J.D.
President

This is the plaque I received from Saint Mary's University.

committed to the importance of making friends beyond the narrow borders of our city, our state, and our nation. We live in a global society, and San Antonio must remain an international city. I smile at the memories of a young Prince Charles greeting adoring high school drum majorettes, President Echeverría and his penchant for presenting lovely gifts, the empress of Iran on the tennis court, and Queen Elizabeth and Prince Philip waving merrily from the *Ms. Lila* barge. I'm gratified to see that San Antonio continues its tradition of hosting international dignitaries and honored to be included at special events that surround those visits.

In the summer of 2018, Mayor Ron Nirenberg and his wife, Erika Propser, and Bexar County Judge Nelson Wolff and his wife, Tracy, hosted the king and queen of Spain during their visit to San Antonio, and I attended a special luncheon in their honor. The royal couple fell in love with our multicultural city, its hospitable and international character, and its wondrous river...just as I did so many years ago.

TWELVE

Summing Up

2018

I see my life as a woven fabric, with many patterns and threads. The most important thread is my family— my strong and loving parents and grandparents, the most wonderful husband imaginable, and children and grandchildren of whom I am very proud.

I was so fortunate to marry a man whose love for me was deep and extraordinary. I loved him in the same way. I still do; our love continues. Sid always knew that family came first for me, and he never felt threatened by my public career. He was an outstanding force in the community, serving for twenty-five years as executive director of the Bexar County Medical Association, and he made many civic contributions through the Alamo Kiwanis Club, the Salvation Army, the Red Cross, the YMCA, and our church.

We watched our girls grow up. Carol graduated

I was fortunate to marry a man whose love for me was deep and extraordinary, and I loved him the same way.

from college in 1967 and Cathy in 1970. They both married, and they both went through a divorce. I had hoped they would experience the same idyllic kind of marriage I had, but I was not living their lives and I recognize that life's journey involves many roads. Fortunately those roads eventually led both Carol and Cathy to second marriages that are strong and right for them.

Carol married Robert Gulley, who had once been

her high school sweetheart at Jefferson High School. They have a daughter, Annalee. Robert is an attorney specializing in environmental and water issues and the author of *Heads Above Water: The Inside Story of the Edwards Aquifer Recovery Implementation Program*, which has become almost a textbook on water use in this part of the country. Carol became a teacher and found her niche working with young people with learning challenges; today she teaches drama and music at San Antonio's Winston School.

Cathy became a flight attendant for American Airlines and married a pilot who was a captain

Robert and Carol Gulley and their daughter, Annalea (*opposite*) and Cathy and John Newton (*left*) are my precious family legacy.

with the airline. They had a son, Dodge, and lived on a small ranch near Decatur, Texas, where Cathy raised Arabian horses. After Cathy divorced, she and Dodge returned to San Antonio. She eventually married John Newton. When they were introduced by mutual friends, John told Cathy she looked familiar. He remembered being a passenger on American Airlines when Cathy was a flight attendant. He had tried to get a date with her, but she was married at the time and turned him down.

I have been blessed with two beloved grandchildren. Like my grandmother Julia, I have taken a real interest in their educations—I think that is what grandmothers do! Annalee majored in political communications at Emerson College in Boston and worked as an intern in Senator Ted Kennedy's office in Washington. She remains deeply interested in political decision-making processes. She lives in Houston and is the director of policy issues and political communication for a company specializing in business and political strategies. Dodge attended college for a while but decided that was not the path for him. He lives in San Antonio and works as a customer service representative for a communications company; he is a wonderful help to me as I navigate life at ninety-six years old.

During these ninety-six years I've seen a lot of change in this world. And during my more than six decades in San Antonio, I've seen this city change and grow into the seventh-largest city in the country. I've witnessed some important milestones in the last sixty years.

Desegregation began during the early years of my civic life, when I was first elected to the city council. There was a national effort to leave old ways behind and to move forward into a new era of race relations. San Antonio chose voluntary desegregation, and we did not experience the ugliness other cities did.

Today, thankfully, it is hard to imagine a segregated society. When young people study that time in history, they are astounded at the idea of public places being designated white only.

In the early 1960s a group of prominent businessmen organized a citizens' committee, headed by James Gaines, a broadcasting executive with the WOAI radio and television stations. Its members called on many privately owned but publicly used places, including restaurants, hotels, theaters, and retail stores, asking them to desegregate. They built enough public support among the city's leading citizens that the owners voluntarily changed their policies. The committee worked quietly and helped pave the way for a desegregation process that went fairly smoothly. History tells us it was far more difficult in other places in the country.

When I entered civic life in San Antonio, the poll tax still existed and city leadership was almost entirely Anglo men. A small Hispanic business sector organized the Mexican American Chamber of Commerce—the humble beginnings of what became the huge and powerful Hispanic Chamber of Commerce of today.

HemisFair 1968 caused major changes as well. It was a wonderful happening; it brought the business community together in new and challenging ways. But when the exposition did not reach its projected revenue levels, some of the companies that had been most supportive in their underwriting experienced losses. Despite its financial troubles, it unified the city in a new way. San Antonio took its place on the national and international stages. Our connections with Latin America blossomed, and the city recognized the potential of its growing tourism industry. Today that industry brings more than 32 million visitors and revenues of more than $13 billion to San Antonio each year.

I have seen tremendous changes in city government. It was not until 1975 that San Antonio's mayor was elected directly by its citizens. Previously the powerful Good Government League selected a slate of candidates for the city council, which in turn chose the mayor. I was the first mayor elected under the new rules. The council members of 1977 were the first to be elected from single-member districts; for the first time every part of our diverse city had a seat at the table. The council evolved from being comprised of only Anglo men to inclusion of some Hispanic business leaders, to inclusion of a woman (me) and an African American, the Rev. Sam James, in 1963. A little more than a decade later, it adopted the system of district representation, and today it is as diverse as San Antonio itself.

Finally I witnessed tremendous changes in San Antonio's economic development, and Gen. Robert McDermott was a major catalyst for that when he arrived in San Antonio in 1968 as the CEO of United Services Automobile Association. It was founded in 1922, the year of my birth, by twenty-five army officers who wanted to insure each other's automobiles. Over its nearly hundred-year history it grew to serve millions of customers and became one of the country's only fully integrated financial services organizations. General McDermott is recognized as a remarkable catalyst, not only for the expanding company but for the overall development of San Antonio. I had introduced him to a young councilman named Henry Cisneros, and they worked well together. When Henry followed me as mayor, they were a combined powerhouse for the city.

The first steps occurred when I became mayor in 1975 and the city's private sector established the San Antonio Economic Development Foundation, chaired by General McDermott. We established a similar department within the city government, and both organizations took a more aggressive role in seeking growth for the city. With time, they became

more and more successful at attracting new businesses, strongly encouraged during Henry's mayoral
terms. Today some of those include energy companies
like Valero and NuStar, manufacturing plants like
Toyota and HOLT CAT, technology companies like
Rackspace and Google, theme parks like SeaWorld
and Fiesta Texas, and a booming medical research
sector that includes the South Texas Medical Center,
the Texas Biomedical Research Institute, and Texas
Research Park.

As one would expect, I've seen changes in myself
over ninety-six years. I found myself progressing
toward feminism. During the years I was growing
up, most of the young women in college with me
looked forward to getting married. The assumption
was that we would marry someone who was nice,
employed, and a good provider. We would become
good wives and mothers and volunteer in the community. All of which I did.

Just before Sid and I were married, in December
1941, the Japanese bombed Pearl Harbor, and the
United States was at war. World War II was a time of
change in America, and women's roles were seen in
a new light. Rosie the Riveter became a symbol for
women, opening new possibilities for us, and I joined
the WAVES. When Sid returned to civilian life, I

was happy as a wife and mother, but I continued to be involved with the world beyond our home. The League of Women Voters brought diverse, challenging issues into my life and was a catalyst for what was ahead for me.

Once we settled in San Antonio, before I entered city government, I experienced a taste of political leadership as president of the PTA at Horace Mann, where my daughters were enrolled. One day after school, Carol told me a funny story. A friend of hers had said, "My dad wonders how your father can afford having your mother be president of the PTA. My mother is only the secretary, and she needs a new dress for every meeting."

If you look back at pictures of me when I was first in office, I am wearing a hat and white gloves, traditional dress for a lady during those times. I registered for my first two city council races as Mrs. S. E. Cockrell Jr. It was not until my third race that I ran as Lila Cockrell. I was first accepted on the council because I was seen as a happily married lady. I was frequently asked to represent the mayor or mayor pro tem at events when they were unavailable. On one of those occasions, I attended a big home builders' event, wearing my hat and gloves, as expected. I was asked to use a hammer to nail something symbolic on a board. As the cameras flashed, I missed the nail and my hat went askew. I was embarrassed when I saw the photos, but men stopped me on the street for days afterward, telling me how cute the photos were. I had behaved according to their concept of women, and they liked that. It was all a gradual progression.

From the beginning I accepted every invitation I received to speak at women's clubs, and I was vigilant in my promotion of women for leadership positions. No doubt my early courses in speech and debate in college helped me tremendously in public life. Not only did I learn to be comfortable at a podium, I also learned how important it is to consider an issue from every angle. I developed a habit I think has stood me well in life. Whenever people come up to me, wanting my support, and tell their story, I never give an instant answer. I let them know that I have heard them and appreciate their information but that I'll need time to make my own study. It's amazing how many times this has saved me from a mistake in life.

I appreciate people—people of all viewpoints— and especially people who have been my friends and helpers along the way. There have been many, from my early school teachers to sorority sisters, to my church community, to dear friends with whom I still attend all sorts of meetings, luncheons, and galas that make life so rich. And, of course, every time I have held a public office, I have had extraordinary assistants and colleagues. Many are mentioned in this story, but because of the time span, I have no doubt missed a few—I am grateful to them all.

Growing up in the Depression probably taught me some important lessons about appreciation. Every family had to cope with changes in lifestyle, some more drastically than others. I remember my mother telling me that there would be setbacks in life, that you can't win them all, and that it is possible to see blessings if you look for them. I find those in the people who care about me and in those memories of my mother making cinnamon toast—instead of fancy scones—to accompany her special tea parties in the 1930s.

Of course, like everyone, I have known sadness. There have been times I have wept, especially at the loss of dear ones like Sid, my mother, my grandfather, and all the others. That is part of the complex extraordinary fabric of life. And I've known incredible joy—life's tapestry is quite remarkable.

Friendship is a very important part of my life. I believe it is essential to human happiness. In my senior years I'm blessed with a circle of very close friends that includes Jane Macon, Rosemary Kowalski, Helen Groves, and Dr. Yvonne Katz. The deaths of dear friends Edith McAllister (at the age of one hundred) and Patsy Steves in 2018, and Amy Freeman Lee in 2004 were a great loss to this community, and to me personally.

I suggest to any young reader—or readers of any age, for that matter—that you devote time to nurturing deep friendships. You will find they amplify your joy in happy times and sustain you in darker times. The mutuality of friendship has been a true blessing as I have moved through my life.

San Antonio's tapestry is still being woven—a work in progress—and I watch that process with pride and hope. I know that I have contributed some of its multicolored threads over the years, and my hope is that our city will continue to grow with grace. We are the fastest-growing city in the country, but there are still large areas of inequality. My dream for our future is that those who have the least can and will continue to embrace opportunities—especially of education—and those who have the most will reach out to less fortunate citizens with love and understanding. The San Antonio River, so graceful in its flow through our community, is my personal symbol of a beautiful tie that binds us together. It

Friendship is essential to human happiness. I was surrounded by friends at my eightieth, ninetieth, and ninety-fifth birthday parties. Top (*left to right*): Former mayors Ed Garza, Howard Peak, Nelson Wolff, and Henry Cisneros. Bottom (*left to right*): Amy Freeman Lee, Edith McAllister, and Rosemary Kowalski.

On the *Ms. Lila* river barge.

lured me to San Antonio so many years ago. I always have loved it, and it continues to make me smile, especially when I see the *Ms. Lila* barge floating by an ever-changing city.

ACKNOWLEDGMENTS

During recent years I have received much encouragement from family and friends to write this memoir, and I am very appreciative of their support and help, as well as their patience, because it has been a long time getting to where I was ready to close the last chapter.

My thanks start with my beloved husband, Sid, whose memory this book is dedicated to, and our two wonderful daughters and their spouses, Carol Ann and Dr. Robert L. Gulley, and Cathy Lynn and John Newton, and my grandchildren, Dodge Sidney Garman and Annalee Earl Gulley. Friends in my adult life who have given much encouragement include Velma Jones (Mrs. L. Bonham Jones), Margaret Lecznar (Mrs. William B. Lecznar), Edith McAllister (Mrs. Walter W. McAllister Jr.), Jane Macon (Mrs. Larry Macon), Rosemary Kowalski, Helen Groves, Deborah Valdez, and Dr. Yvonne Katz. My appreciation also goes to all of my former colleagues on the city council, with special thanks to the Hon. Henry G. Cisneros, who was so generous in his remarks in the foreword to this book, and to his wife, Mary Alice; to Norma Rodriguez, our beloved city clerk emeritus; and to the late Shirl Thomas, my executive assistant in those years I served as mayor.

Special thanks as well go to another good friend, Bexar County judge Nelson Wolff, and his wife, Tracy, and to Sylvia Rodriguez, former county auditor, who just kept after me to finish the book! I wish to thank Alice Helmick for her assistance at my home in helping me find pictures and documents for inclusion in this book, and Sherry Wagner, who assisted in making valued suggestions in my earlier effort at completion of the book. My final thanks go to Catherine Nixon Cooke, who collaborated with me in the last big push to complete the book and get it published. I hope that you, dear reader, find it enjoyable—and good for a few big chuckles!

Trinity University Press gratefully acknowledges the generosity of these individuals and organizations for their financial support of this publication:

Carri Baker
Dr. Alfonso and Mary Alice Chiscano
Henry and Mary Alice Cisneros
Evangelina G. Flores
Frost Bank
Don Frost
Cathy Obriotti Green
Berto Guerra
Jimmy Hasslocher
Edward Sterlin Holmesy
Linebarger, Goggal, Blair & Simpson, LLP
Nancy Loeffler
Jane H. Macon
Richard Perez
Dr. Carl E. Raba Jr.
Norma Rodriguez

LILA COCKRELL's life in public service spans more than six decades. She was elected to San Antonio's city council in 1963 and served three terms, followed by four terms as mayor. She is a graduate of Southern Methodist University and holds honorary degrees from her alma mater and from the Alamo Community Colleges, Our Lady of the Lake University, and St. Mary's University. She served as an ensign in the WAVES during World War II and later as president of the League of Women Voters in Dallas and San Antonio, executive director of United San Antonio, chair of the San Antonio River Oversight Committee, director of the San Antonio Parks Foundation, and in many other civic leadership positions. In addition to her achievements in public life, she has cherished her role as wife, mother, and grandmother.

CATHERINE NIXON COOKE is the author of *Juan O'Gorman: A Confluence of Civilizations* and *Powering a City: How Energy and Big Dreams Transformed San Antonio,* both published by Trinity University Press; *The Thistle and the Rose: Romance, Railroads, and Big Oil in Revolutionary Mexico;* and *Tom Slick, Mystery Hunter,* which is in development as a major motion picture. She is a contributor to two anthologies, *They Lived to Tell the Tale: True Stories of Modern Adventure from the Legendary Explorers Club* and *Adventurous Dreams, Adventurous Lives.* She and her husband divide their time between San Antonio, the Texas hill country, and more remote parts of the world where untold stories beckon.